THE 7 LAWS OF TEACHING

John Milton Gregory

 Baker Books

A Division of Baker Book House Co
Grand Rapids, Michigan 49516

Reprinted by Baker Books
a division of Baker Book House Company
P.O. Box 6287, Grand Rapids, MI 49516-6287

New paperback edition 1995

ISBN: 0-8010-5272-6

Fourth printing, October 1997

Printed in the United States of America

For information about academic books, resources
for Christian leaders,and all new releases available
from Baker Book House, visit our web site:
            http://www.bakerbooks.com/

THE 7 LAWS OF TEACHING

PREFATORY NOTE

The Seven Laws of Teaching was first published in 1884. Extensive changes were made in 1917 by William C. Bagley and Warren K. Layton, both of the School of Education at the University of Illinois. However, every effort was made to retain both the form and substance of the original. Baker Book House first reprinted this revised edition in 1954. Frequent reprintings point to the timelessness of the content of *The Seven Laws of Teaching.*

JOHN MILTON GREGORY

The author of this book, John Milton Gregory, was one of the educational leaders of the generation that has just passed from the stage. He was born at Sand Lake, in Rensselaer County, New York, on July 6th, 1822. His early training was obtained in the district schools and he became himself a district-school teacher at the age of seventeen. Three years later, apparently destined for the profession of law, he entered Union College at Schenectady, New York, but after graduating in 1846, he gave up the study of law to enter the ministry of the Baptist Church. His heart, however, was in teaching, and in 1852 he became head of a classical school in Detroit, Michigan. Almost immediately he was recognized as a leader in the educational councils of the state. He was active in the affairs of the State Teachers' Association and was one of the founders and the first editor of the "Michigan Journal of Education." His intimate knowledge of educational affairs and his popularity among the teachers led to his election in 1858 to the State superintendency of public instruction, an office to which he was twice reelected. He declined a fourth nomination in 1864 when, as president of Kalamazoo College, he entered upon a new phase of his career — the organization of institutions for higher education.

In 1868, when the University of Illinois was established under the name, "Illinois State Industrial University," Dr. Gregory was asked to undertake the organization of the new institution. His work for thirteen years in laying the foundation of one of the largest and strongest of the state universities gives him a secure place in the history of American education. After leaving the University of Illinois he served for some time as a member of the United States Civil Service Commission. The great work of his life, however, was the organization of the University, and just before he died in 1898 he asked that his body be laid to rest within the campus of the school for which he had done so much. This request was reverently complied with.

Dr. Gregory's book, "The Seven Laws of Teaching," was first published in 1884. A clear and simple statement of the important factors governing the art of teaching, it has been especially successful as a handbook for Sunday school teachers. In recognition of Dr. Gregory's great service to the University of Illinois, two members of the School of Education undertook the revision of the book which is here presented.

INTRODUCTION

Let us, like the Master, carefully observe a little child, that we may learn from him what education is; for education, in its broadest meaning, embraces all the steps and processes by which an infant is gradually transformed into a full-grown and intelligent man.

Let us take account of the infant. He has a complete human body, with eyes, hands, and feet — and all the organs of sense, of action, and of locomotion — and yet he lies helpless in his cradle. He laughs, cries, feels; he has the attributes of the adult, but not the powers.

In what does this infant differ from a man? Simply in being a child. His body and limbs are small, weak, and without voluntary use. His feet cannot walk; his hands have no skill; his lips cannot speak. His eyes see without perceiving, and his ears hear without understanding. The universe into which he has come lies around him unknown and mysterious.

More observation and study make it clear to us that the child is but a germ—he has not his destined growth—and he is ignorant—without acquired ideas.

On these two facts rest the two notions of education: (1) the development of capacities, and (2) the acquisition of experience. The first is the maturing of body and mind to full growth and strength; the second is the process of furnishing the child with the heritage of the race.

Each of these facts—the child's immaturity and his ignorance—might serve as a basis for a science of education. The first would emphasize the capacities of the human being, their order of development and their laws of growth and action. The second would involve a study of the various branches of human knowledge, and how they are discovered, developed, and perfected. Each of these sciences would necessarily involve the other, as a study of powers involves a knowledge of their products, and a study of effects includes a survey of causes.

Based upon these two forms of educational science, we find the art of education to be a two-fold one: the art of *training* and the art of *teaching*.

Since the child is immature in the use of all his capacities it is the first business of education to give such training as will bring them to full development. This training may be physical, mental, or moral.

Since the child is ignorant, it is the business of education to communicate to it the experience of the race. This is properly the work of teaching. Considered in this light, the school is but one of the agencies of education, since we continue throughout our lives to acquire experience. The first object of teaching, then, is to stimulate in the pupil the love of learning, and to form in him habits and ideals of independent study.

These two, the cultivation of capacities and the transmission of experience, together make up the teacher's work. All organizing and governing are subsidiary of this two-fold aim. The result to be sought is a full-grown physical, intellectual, and moral manhood, with such resources as are necessary to make life useful and happy and as will enable the individual to go on learning from all the activities of life.

These two great branches of the educational art — training and teaching — though separable in thought, are not separable in practice. We can only train by teaching, and we teach best when we train best. The proper training of the intellectual capacities is found in the acquisition, elaboration, and application of the knowledge and skills which represent the heritage of the race.

There is, however, a practical advantage in keeping these two processes of education before the mind. The teacher with these clearly in view will observe more easily and estimate more intelligently the real progress of his pupils. He will not be content with a dry daily drill which keeps his pupils at work as in a treadmill, nor will he be satisfied with cramming their minds with useless facts and names. He will carefully note both sides of his pupils' education, and will direct his labors and adapt his lessons wisely and skilfully to secure both of the ends in view.

This statement of the two sides of the science and art of education brings us to the point of view from which may be clearly seen the real aim of this little volume. That aim is stated in its title—THE SEVEN LAWS OF TEACHING. Its object is to set forth, in a certain systematic order, the principles of the art of teaching. It deals with mental capacities only as they need to be considered in a clear discussion of the work of acquiring experience in the process of education.

As the most obvious work of the schoolroom is that of studying the various branches of knowledge, so the work of teaching—the work of assigning, explaining, and hearing lessons—is that which chiefly occupies the time and attention of the instructor. To explain the laws of teaching will, therefore, seem the most direct and practical way to instruct teachers in their art. It presents at once the clearest and most practical view of their duties, and of the methods by which they may win success in their work. Having learned the laws of teaching, the teacher will easily master the philosophy of training.

This little book does not claim to set forth the whole science of education, nor even the whole art of teaching. But if it has succeeded in grouping around the seven factors, which are present in every instance of true teaching, the leading principles and rules of the teaching art, so that they can be seen in their natural order and relations, and can be methodically learned and used, it has fulfilled the desire of the author.

CONTENTS

The Laws of Teaching

1. Teaching has its natural laws as fixed as the laws of the planets or of growing organisms. It is a process in which definite forces are employed to produce definite results, and these results follow as regularly and certainly as the day follows the sun. What the teacher does, he does through natural agencies working out their natural effects. Causation is as certain—if not always so obvious nor so easily understood—in the movements of mind as in those of matter. The laws of mind are as fixed as material laws.

2. To discover the laws of any process, whether of mind or of matter, makes it possible to bring that process under the control of one who knows the laws and can command the conditions. Knowledge of the laws. of electric currents has made it possible to send messages through the ocean; and he who masters the laws of teaching may convey to the minds of others the experience of the race. He who would gain harvests must obey nature's laws for the growing of corn, and he who would teach a child successfully must follow the laws of teaching. Nowhere, in the world of mind or in the world of matter, can man produce any effects except as he employs the means upon which those effects depend.

3. Teaching, in its simplest sense, is the communication of experience. This experience may consist of facts, truths, doctrines, ideas, or ideals, or it may consist of the processes or skills of an art. It may be taught by the use of words, by signs, by objects, by actions, or by examples; but whatever the substance, the mode, or the aim of the teaching, the act itself, fundamentally considered, is always substantially the same: it is a communication of experience. It is painting in the mind of another the picture in one's own— the shaping of the thought and understanding to the comprehension of some truth which the teacher knows and wishes to communicate. Further on we shall see that the word "communication" is used here, not in the sense of the transmission of a mental something from one person to another, but rather in the sense of helping another to reproduce the same experience and thus to make it common to the two.

The Seven Factors **4.** To discover the law of any phenomenon, we must subject that phenomenon to a scientific analysis and study its separate parts. If any complete act of teaching be so analyzed, it will be found to contain seven distinct elements or factors: (1) two personal factors—a teacher and a learner; (2) two mental factors—a common language or medium of communication, and a lesson or truth or art to be communicated; and (3) three functional acts or processes—that of the teacher, that of the learner, and a final or finishing process to test and fix the result.

5. These are essential elements in every full and complete act of teaching. Whether the lesson be a single fact told in three minutes, or a lecture occupying as many hours, the seven factors are all present, if the work is effective. None of them can be omitted, and no others need be added. If there is a true science of teaching, it must be found in the laws and relations of these seven factors.

6. To discover their laws, let us pass the seven factors again in careful review: (1) a teacher; (2) a learner; (3) a common language or medium of communication; (4) a lesson or truth; (5) the teacher's work; (6) the learner's work; (7) the review work, which organizes, applies, perfects, and fastens the work which has been done. Each of these seven factors is distinguished from the rest by some essential characteristics; each is a distinct entity or fact of nature. Since every fact of nature is the product and proof of some law of nature, each element here described has its own great law of function, and these taken together constitute The Seven Laws of Teaching.

7. It may seem trivial so to insist upon all this. Some will say: "Of course there can be no teaching without a teacher and a pupil, without a language and a lesson, and unless the teacher teaches and the learner learns; or, finally, without a proper review, if any assurance is to be gained that the work has been successful. All this is too obvious to need assertion." So also is it obvious that when seeds, soil, heat, light, and moisture come together in proper measure, plants are produced and grow to the harvest; but the obviousness of these common facts does not prevent their hiding among them some of the most profound and mysterious laws of nature. So, too, a simple act of teaching may hide within it some of the most potent and significant laws of mental life.

The Laws Stated   **8.** These laws are not obscure and hard to reach. They are so simple and natural that they suggest themselves almost spontaneously to the careful observer. They lie imbedded in the simplest description that can be given of the seven elements named, as in the following:

(1) A *teacher* must be one who *knows* the lesson or truth or art to be taught.

(2) A *learner* is one who *attends* with interest to the lesson.

(3) The *language* used as a *medium* between teacher and learner must be *common* to both.

(4) The *lesson* to be mastered must be explicable in the terms of truth already known by the learner—the *unknown* must be explained by means of the *known.*

(5) *Teaching* is *arousing* and *using* the *pupil's mind* to grasp the desired thought or to master the desired art.

(6) *Learning* is *thinking* into one's own *understanding* a new idea or truth or working into *habit* a new art or skill.

(7) The *test and proof* of teaching done— the finishing and fastening process—must be a *reviewing, rethinking, reknowing, reproducing,* and *applying* of the material that has been taught, the knowledge and ideals and arts that have been communicated.

9. These definitions and statements are perhaps so simple and obvious as to need no argument or proof; but their force as fundamental laws may be more clearly seen if they are stated as rules for teaching. Addressed to the teacher, they may read as follows:

The Laws Stated as Rules

(1) Know thoroughly and familiarly the lesson you wish to teach—teach from a full mind and a clear understanding.

(2) Gain and keep the attention and interest

of the pupils upon the lesson. Do not try to teach without attention.

(3) Use words understood in the same way by the pupils and yourself—language clear and vivid to both.

(4) Begin with what is already well known to the pupil upon the subject and with what he has himself experienced—and proceed to the new material by single, easy, and natural steps, letting the known explain the unknown.

(5) Stimulate the pupil's own mind to action. Keep his thought as much as possible ahead of your expression, placing him in the attitude of a discoverer, an anticipator.

(6) Require the pupil to reproduce in thought the lesson he is learning—thinking it out in its various phases and applications till he can express it in his own language.

(7) *Review, review, review,* reproducing the old, deepening its impression with new thought, linking it with added meanings, finding new applications, correcting any false views, and completing the true.

Essentials of Successful Teaching

10. These rules, and the laws upon which they are based, underlie and govern all successful teaching. If taken in their broadest significance, nothing need be added to them or taken away. No one who thoroughly masters and uses them need fail as a teacher, if he also has qualities that enable him properly to maintain the good order necessary to give them free and undisturbed action. Disorder, noise, and confusion may hinder and prevent the results desired, just as the constant disturbance of some chemical elements forbids the formation of the compounds which the laws of chemistry would otherwise produce. But good teaching, in itself, will often bring about good order.

11. Like all the great laws of nature, these laws of teaching seem clear and obvious; but like other fundamental truths, their simplicity is more apparent than real. Each law varies in its applications with varying minds and persons, although remaining constant in itself; and each stands related to other laws and facts till it reaches the outermost limits of the art of teaching. In the succeeding chapters we shall proceed to a careful study of these seven laws, reaching in our discussion many valuable principles in education and many practical rules which can be of use in the teacher's work.

12. These laws and rules apply to the teaching of all subjects in all grades, since they are the fundamental conditions on which ideas may pass from one mind to another. They are as valid and useful for the instructor in the university as for the teacher in the elementary school, and for the teaching of a law in logic as for instruction in arithmetic.

13. There may be many successful teachers who never heard of these laws, and who do not *consciously* follow them; just as there are people who walk safely without any theoretical knowledge of gravitation, and talk intelligibly without studying grammar. Like the musician who plays "by ear," these "natural" teachers have learned from practice the laws of teaching, and obey them from habit. It is none the less true that their success comes from obeying law, and not in spite of law.

Skill and Enthusiasm

14. Let no one fear that a study of the laws of teaching will tend to substitute a cold, mechanical sort of work for the warmhearted, enthusiastic teaching so much to be desired, and so much admired and praised. True skill kindles and keeps alive enthusiasm by giving it success where it would otherwise be discouraged by defeat. The true worker's love for his work grows with his ability to do it well. Enthusiasm will accomplish all the more when guided by intelligence and armed with skill.

15. Unreflecting superintendents and school boards often prefer enthusiastic teachers to those who are simply well educated or experienced. They believe, not without reason, that enthusiasm will accomplish more with inadequate learning and little skill than the best-trained and most erudite teacher wholly lacking in zeal. But why choose either the ignorant enthusiast or the educated sluggard? Enthusiasm is not confined to the unskilled and the ignorant, nor are all calm, cool men idlers. There is an enthusiasm born of skill— a joy in doing what one can do well—that is far more effective, where art is involved, than the enthusiasm born in vivid feeling. The steady advance of veterans is more powerful than the mad rush of raw recruits. The world's best work, in the schools as in the shops, is done by the calm, steady, and persistent efforts of skilled workmen who know how to keep their tools sharp, and to make every effort reach its mark.

16. The most serious objection to systematic teaching, based on the laws of teaching, has sometimes come from pastors, Sunday school teachers, and others, who have assumed that the principal aim of the Sunday school is to impress rather than to instruct; and that skilful teaching, if desirable at all, is much less important than warm appeals to the feelings and earnest exhortations on the proper occasions. But what exhortation will have such permanent power as that which is heralded by some clear truth? If the choice must be between the warmhearted teacher who makes gushing appeals, and the coldhearted one who stifles all feeling by his indifference, the former is perhaps to be preferred; but why either? Is there no healthful mean between steam and ice for the water of life? The teacher whose own mind glows with the truth, and who skilfully leads his pupils to a clear understanding of the same truth, will not fail in inspirational power.

17. These questions may be left to call forth their own inevitable answers. They will have served their purpose if they repel the disposition to discredit the need of true *teaching* in Sunday schools as well in day schools; and if they convince Sunday school leaders that the laws of teaching are the laws of mind, which must be followed as faithfully in studying the Word of God as in studying His works.

A Word to Teachers

18. Leaving to other chapters the full discussion of the meaning and philosophy of those seven laws, we here urge the teacher, especially the Sunday school teacher, to give them the most serious attention. While facing your pupils, how often have you wished for the power to look into their minds, and to plant there with sure hand some truth of science or some belief of the gospel? No key will ever open to you the doors of those chambers in which live your pupils' souls; no glass will ever enable you to penetrate their mysterious gloom. But in the great laws of your common nature lie the lines of communication by which you may send the thought fresh from your mind, and awaken the other to receive and embrace it.

19. In the discussion of these laws there will necessarily occur some seeming repetitions. They are like seven hilltops of different height scattered over a common territory. As we climb each in succession, many points in the landscapes seen ferent views, but always in a new light and with from their summits will be found included in dif- a fresh horizon. New groupings will show new relations and bring to light, for the careful student, new aspects and uses. The repetitions themselves will not be useless, as they will serve to emphasize the most important features of the art of teaching, and will impress upon teachers those principles which demand the most frequent attention.

The Law of the Teacher

1. The universal reign of law is the central truth of modern science. No force in man or nature but works under the control of law; no effect in mind or matter but is produced in conformity with law. The simplest notion of natural law is that nature remains forever uniform in its forces and operations. Causes compel their effects, and effects obey their causes, by irresistible laws. Things are what they are by reason of the laws of their being, and to learn the law of any fact is to learn the most fundamental truth that we can know about it. This uniformity of nature is the basis of all science and of all practical art. In mind and in matter the reign of unvarying laws is the primal condition of any true science. The mind has freedom within law but no liberty to produce effects contrary to laws. The teacher is therefore as much the subject of law as the star that shines or the ship that sails. Many qualifications are recognized as important to the teacher's position and work; and if all the requirements sought for could be obtained, the teacher would be a model man or

woman, a perfect assemblage of impossible ex-
cellences. Good character and rare moral qualities are desirable in an instructor of the young,
if not for his actual work, at least to prevent harm
from his example; but if, one by one, we dismiss
from our catalogue of needful qualifications for
the work of teaching those not absolutely indispensable, we shall find ourselves obliged to retain
at last, as necessary to the very notion of teaching,
a knowledge of the subject matter to be taught.
The Law of the Teacher, then—the law which
limits and describes him—is this: *The teacher
must know that which he would teach.*

**The Philosophy
of the Law**

2. That we cannot teach without knowledge
seems too simple for proof. How can something
come out of nothing, or how can darkness give
light? To affirm this law seems like declaring a
truism: but deeper study shows it to be a fundamental truth—the law of the teacher. No other
qualification is so fundamental and essential. If
the terms of the law are reversed, another important truth is revealed: *What the teacher knows
he must teach.*

3. The word *know* stands central in the law of
the teacher. *Knowledge* is the material with which
the teacher works, and the first reason for the law
must be sought in the nature of knowledge. What
men call knowledge is of all degrees, from the
first glimpse of truth to the full understanding. At

different stages the experience of the race, as we acquire it, is characterized by: (1) faint recognition; (2) the ability to recall for ourselves, or to describe in a general way to others, what we have learned; (3) the power readily to explain, prove, illustrate, and apply it; and (4) such knowledge and appreciation of the truth in its deeper significance and wider relations, that by the force of its importance we *act* upon it—our *conduct* is modified by it. History is history only to him who thus reads and knows it. It is this last form of knowledge, or experience, which must be read into the law of the true teacher.

4. It is not affirmed that no one can teach at all without this fulness of knowledge; nor is it true that every one who knows his subject matter thus thoroughly will necessarily teach successfully. But imperfect knowing must be reflected in imperfect teaching. What a man does not know he cannot teach successfully. But the law of the teacher is only one of the laws of teaching, and failure may come from the violations of other conditions as well as from neglect of this. Likewise success in some measure may come from obedience to the other laws. However, teaching must be uncertain and limping when characterized by an inadequate knowledge of the material to be taught.

5. A truth is known by its resemblances, and can best be seen in the light of other truths. The pupil, instead of seeing a fact alone, should see it linked to the great body of truth, in all its fruitful relations. Great principles are discovered amid familiar facts vividly seen, and concepts clearly wrought. The power of illustration—a most important tool in the teacher's art—comes only out of clear and familiar knowledge. The unknowing teacher is like the blind trying to lead the blind with only an empty lamp to light the way.

6. Consider the common facts taught in the geography of the schools—the roundness of the earth, the extent of oceans and continents, mountains, rivers, and peopled states and cities— how tame and slight in interest to the half-taught teacher and his pupils; but how inspiring as seen by the Herschels, the Danas, and the Guyots! To them appear in vision the long processions of age-filling causes which have given shape to the globe. To such teachers geography is one chapter in the science and history of the universe. So, too, with Biblical truths; they are meager in meaning to the careless reader and to the nonstudious teacher, but they are brilliant with truth and rich with meaning to those who bring to their study the converging lights of history, science, and indeed all forms of recorded experience.

7. But the law of the teacher goes deeper still. Truth must be clearly understood before it can be vividly felt. Only the true students of any science grow enthusiastic over it. It is the clearness of their vision which inspires the wonderful eloquence of the poet and the orator, and makes them the teachers of their race. It was Hugh Miller, the geologist, whose eye deciphered and whose pen recorded "The Testimony of the Rocks." Kepler, the great astronomer, grew wild as the mysteries of the stars unrolled before him, and Agassiz could not afford time to lecture for money while absorbed in the study of the fishes of an ancient world. That teacher will be cold and lifeless who only half knows the subject he would teach; but one fired with enthusiasm will unconsciously inspire his pupils with his own interest.

8. This earnest feeling of truths clearly conceived is the secret of the enthusiasm so much admired and praised in teacher and preacher. Common truths become transformed for such a teacher. History becomes a living panorama; geography swells out into great continental stretches of peopled nations; astronomy becomes the march of worlds and world systems. How can the teacher's manner fail to be earnest and inspiring when his subject matter is so rich in radiant reality?

9. While knowledge thus thoroughly and familiarly mastered rouses into higher action all the powers of the teacher, it also gives him the command and use of those powers. Instead of a feeling of subservience to his textbook, the teacher who knows his lesson as he ought is at home in his recitation, and can watch the efforts of his class and direct with ease the trend of their thoughts. He is ready to recognize and interpret their first glimpses of truth; to remove the obstacles from their path, and to aid and encourage them.

10. A teacher's ready and evident knowledge helps to give the pupil needed confidence. We follow with expectation and delight the guide who has a thorough knowledge of the field we wish to explore, but we follow reluctantly and without interest the ignorant and incompetent leader. Children object to being taught by one in whom they have no confidence. And this is not all. The great scholars—the Newtons, the Humboldts, and the Huxleys—kindle public interest in the sciences in which they themselves are working; in the same way the well-prepared teacher awakens in his pupils the active desire to study further. In some unfortunate cases, great knowledge is unaccompanied by the ability to inspire pupils with a love of study, and this is a condition fatal to successful teaching, especially with young pupils. Better a teacher with limited knowledge but with the power to stimulate his pupils, than an Agassiz without it.

11. Such is the philosophy of this first great law of teaching. Thus understood, it clearly portrays the splendid ideal which no one except the Great

Teacher ever fully realized, but which every true teacher must approach. It defines accurately the forces with which the successful teacher must go to his work. From the mother teaching her little child, to the instructor of the most abstract science, the orator addressing senates, and the preacher teaching great congregations, this law knows no exceptions and permits no successful violations. It affirms everywhere, *the teacher must know that which he would teach.*

12. Among the rules which arise out of the Law of the Teacher, the following are the most important:

Rules for Teachers

(1) Prepare each lesson by fresh study. Last year's knowledge has necessarily faded somewhat. Only fresh conceptions inspire us to our best efforts.

(2) Find in the lesson its analogies to more familiar facts and principles. In these lie the illustrations by which it may be taught to others.

(3) Study the lesson until it takes shape in familiar language. The final product of clear thought is clear speech.

(4) Find the natural order of the several steps of the lesson. In every science there is a natural path from the simplest notions to the broadest views; so, too, in every lesson.

(5) Find the relation of the lesson to the lives of the learners. Its practical value lies in these relations.

(6) Use freely all legitimate aids, but never rest until the real understanding is clearly before you.

(7) Bear in mind that complete mastery of a few things is better than an ineffective smattering of many.

(8) Have a definite time for the study of each lesson, in advance of the teaching. All things help the duty done on time. One keeps on learning the lesson studied in advance, and gathers fresh interest and illustrations.

(9) Have a plan of study, but do not hesitate, when necessary, to study beyond the plan. The best mnemonic device is to ask and answer these questions about the lesson: What? How? Why?

(10) Do not deny yourself the help of good books on the subject of your lessons. Buy, borrow, or beg, if necessary, but obtain somehow the help of the best thinkers, enough at least to stimulate your own thought; but do not read without thinking. If possible, talk the lesson over with an intelligent friend; collision often brings light. In the absence of these aids, write your views; expressing your thoughts in writing may clear them of obscurities.

Violations and Mistakes

13. This discussion would be incomplete without some mention of the frequent violations of the law. The best teacher may spoil his most careful and earnest work by thoughtless blunders. The true teacher will make as few errors as possible, and will profit by those that he makes.

(1) The very ignorance of his pupils may tempt the teacher to neglect careful preparation and study. He may think that in any event he will know much more of the lesson than the pupils can, and imagine that he will find something to say about it, or that the ignorance will pass unnoticed. A sad mistake, and one that often costs dearly. The cheat is almost sure to be discovered, and from that time the teacher's standing with the class is gone.

(2) Some teachers assume that it is the pupils' work, not theirs, to study the lesson, and that with the aid of the book in hand, they will be able easily to ascertain whether the pupils have done their duty. Better let one of the pupils who knows his lesson examine the others, than to discourage study by your own indifference and lack of preparation. Teaching is not merely "hearing lessons."

(3) Others look hastily through the lesson, and conclude that though they have not thoroughly mastered it, or perhaps any part of it, they have gathered enough to fill the period, and can, if necessary, supplement the little they know with random talk or story. Or, lacking time or heart for any preparation, they dismiss all thought of teaching, fill the hour with such exercises as may occur to them, and hope that, as the school is a good

thing anyway, the pupils will receive some benefit from mere attendance.

(4) A more serious fault is that of those who, failing to find stimulation in the lesson, make it a mere framework upon which to hang some fancies of their own.

(5) There is a meaner wrong done by the teacher who seeks to conceal his lazy ignorance with some pompous pretense of learning, hiding his lack of knowledge by an array of high-sounding phrases beyond the comprehension of his pupils, uttering solemn platitudes in a wise tone, or claiming extensive study and profound information which he has not the time to lay properly before them. Who has not seen these shams practiced upon pupils?

14. Thus many teachers go to their work either partly prepared or wholly unprepared. They are like messengers without a message. They lack entirely the power and enthusiasm necesssary to produce the fruits which we have a right to look for from their efforts. Let this first fundamental law of teaching be thoroughly obeyed, and our schools will increase in numbers and in usefulness.

The Law of the Learner

1. Passing from the teacher to the pupil, our next inquiry is for the *Law of the Learner.* Here the search must be for those characteristics which differentiate the learner from other persons—for the essential elements which make him a learner. Let us place before us a successful student, and note carefully his actions and qualities. His intent look and absorbed manner are signs of his interest and attention. Interest and attention characterize the mental state of the true learner, and constitute the essential basis on which the process of learning rests. The law of the learner, then, may be stated as follows: *The learner must attend with interest to the material to be learned.*

2. The law thus stated may seem to be a truism, but it is as really profound as it is seemingly simple. The plainest proof of its truth lies in the readiness with which every one will admit it. Its real significance can be found by careful study.

3. Attention means the direction of the mind upon some object. The object may be external,

Attention Described

as when one watches carefully the operation of a machine or listens intently to a piece of music; or it may be mental, as when one "calls to mind" some past experience, or "reflects" upon the meaning of some idea. The psychologist speaks of this direction of the mind as the act of bringing the object into the "focus" of consciousness. Consciousness is thus thought of as presenting a "focus" and a "margin." The focus is occupied by our awareness of the object that is being "attended" to, the margin by those sensations and feelings that are still within the range of consciousness, but which are vague, indistinct, and not clearly defined.

4. Attention, then, is not a constant and invariable condition. When we speak of "concentrated" or "absorbed" attention we mean that the object attended to is occupying the whole of consciousness. But one may attend with varying degrees of absorption or concentration. One may let one's mind flit from this object to that, following each passing stimulus for a moment or two until something else "catches the attention"; or one may hold oneself resolutely to a certain object and still be "aware" that other objects are tempting one in other directions; or one may become so completely absorbed in a given object that all other objects are practically nonexistent so far as consciousness is concerned.

5. There are, then, three different kinds of attention, each of which is important from the point of view of teaching and learning.

(1) Attention of the "flitting" kind is often called "passive" attention, because it involves no effort of will. One simply follows the behest of the strongest stimulus; one is "passive" because one is letting the forces that play about him control the mental life. This is the primitive, instinctive, basic type of attention—the attention of every one at some times during the day, especially when one is tired or when one is in a playful mood; but particularly the attention of the little child.

(2) But the essential characteristic of the human mind is that it can control, rather than be controlled by, the forces that surround it. It can rise above its immediate environment and look beyond the present into the future. It can even attend *away from* objects that naturally attract attention and hold itself persistently and resolutely to tasks and duties that are not immediately attractive but which it recognizes as important and worthy and necessary. It can hold momentary fancy in leash and work resolutely and persistently toward a remote goal. This distinctively human type of attention is called "active" attention because its first condition is an effort of the will, a determination to do what should be done in spite of allurements to do something else that is pleasanter and more attractive.

(3) But attention of this effortful, active sort is not always or often the most economical

and effective for learning. Generally speaking we learn most easily and most economically when we are "absorbed" in our work, when the objects that we are trying to fix in mind and remember permanently really attract us in their own right, so to speak—when our learning is so fascinating that it simply "carries us with it." Attention of this sort frequently grows out of persistent effort—out of what we have just termed "active" attention. This attention resembles passive attention in that its object is always attractive in itself and demands little or no effort to be brought into the focus of consciousness; but it also grows out of active attention, out of effort and persistence; this third type of attention is consequently termed "secondary passive" attention.

6. It is obvious that attention of the secondary passive type is, from the learner's point of view, the most desirable to cultivate. It means economy of learning, it means pleasant learning, it means effective learning. But the general verdict of human experience is that these most desirable conditions are not easily fulfilled—if they were, indeed, there would be little need for either teachers or schools. It seems to be generally true that these sustained and abiding "interests" are to be purchased only at a price—and the price is strenuous effort. One cannot lay this down as an unvarying rule, for there are doubtless some worthy interests that are "grown into" with little effort—

almost by following the lines of least resistance. This is possible—but it is also possible that a ship which is left to the mercy of every wind that blows *may* be wafted ultimately into some safe and profitable harbor. Human experience during the long ages has taught few lessons that are more dependable than that which predicates effort, sacrifice, and persistence as the chief ingredients of success, and this holds as generally of success in learning as it does of success in business, art, invention, and industry. The man who simply drifts into success in any field of human activity is almost as rare as the ship that drifts aimlessly into a safe harbor; certainly those who know well and know thoroughly have paid the price of mental toil and mental effort for their mastery—and mental toil and mentai effort are only other words for active attention.

7. It would be folly, however, for the teacher to interpret this need of effort upon the part of the learner as meaning that the art of teaching consists only of setting tasks and driving pupils to the accomplishment of these tasks—for it is also agreed that the kind of effort that comes from the incitement of driving or the incentive of fear is quite unlikely to develop these permanent and abiding interests. Thousands if not millions of pupils under such treatment have never got beyond the stage of active attention; more than this, they have developed a distinct and permanent dislike for what they have tried to learn. The duty of the teacher is essentially not that of a driver or a taskmaster but rather that of a counselor and guide. His aim must be to develop secondary passive attention. The best way to do this is to make the stages of advancement gradual, so that while the pupil must put forth effort in grasping each new step in the lesson or in the series of lessons, the completion of each step will also make the effort seem worthwhile.

8. Modern theories of teaching emphasize the importance of "problems" in insuring this progressive series of efforts, and there is much to commend in this movement. The theory is that, if you can interest the pupil in solving a problem, he will put forth the effort necessary to grasp the knowledge which is essential to the solution. Thus if the knowledge that one wishes to teach can be organized with reference to these problems, the learning, it is maintained, will really take care of itself.

9. As an example of this "problem method" of teaching as exemplified in Sunday school work, one may take the general topic, the geography of Palestine. The traditional method of teaching would consider this topic as an information-unit. Palestine would be located with reference to its place on the globe, and with reference to the adjacent countries; its natural features would be described—its mountains, plains, seas, and rivers;

the climate would be referred to and perhaps explained by the various factors of latitude, altitude, prevailing winds, neighborhood of bodies of water, deserts, etc.; the productions and the people would be considered in conclusion. But the problem method would start in another way. An effort might be made to interest the pupils in an imaginary journey to Palestine. How they would reach the country, how they would live and travel while there, how the people lived and worked and dressed—all of these and many other subordinate problems would create what might be called a "natural" demand for the information which, under the older method, would be presented systematically and somewhat abstractly.

10. There is an important place for the problem method in teaching, but it is clear that it cannot entirely replace systematic and progressive study. Its value lies chiefly in bringing about an initial momentum for learning. The method should also be used as a stimulating variant, breaking the monotony of a too logical and abstract procedure. Most children, once they have gained a start in study, will be able and willing to work systematically. Everything depends upon the skill with which the teacher passes from step to step, linking the new with the old, and gradually building up a whole that is composed of well-articulated parts.

11. However much teachers may neglect it in practice, they readily admit that without attention

The Philosophy of the Law

the pupil cannot learn. One may as well talk to the deaf or to the dead as to attempt to teach a child who is wholly inattentive. All this may seem perhaps too obvious to need discussion, but a brief survey of the facts which underlie the law will make clear its force and authority.

12. Knowledge cannot be passed like a material substance from one mind to another, for thoughts are not objects which may be held and handled. Ideas can be communicated only by inducing in the receiving mind processes corresponding to those by which these ideas were first conceived. Ideas must be rethought, experience must be re-experienced. It is obvious, therefore, that something more is required than a mere presentation; the pupil must think. He must work with a fixed aim and purpose—in other words, with attention. It is not enough to look and listen. If the mind is only half aroused, the conceptions gained will be faint and fragmentary—as inaccurate and useless as they are fleeting. Teacher and textbook may be full of information but the learner will get from them only so much as his power of attention enables him to shape in his own mind.

13. The notion that the mind is only a receptacle in which to stow other people's ideas is entirely incorrect. The nature of mind, as far as we can understand it, is that of a power, or force, actuated by motives. The striking clock may sound in the ear, and the passing object may paint its image in the eye, but the inattentive mind neither hears nor sees. Who has not read a whole page with the eyes, and at the bottom found himself unable to recall a single idea that it contained? The senses had done their work, but the mind had been busy with other thoughts.

14. The vigor of mental action, like that of muscular action, is proportioned to the stimulus which inspires it. The pupil's mind may not at once respond to the command of the teacher, nor to the call of a cold sense of duty. It is only when we begin our work "with a will"—that is, with interest in our work—that we are working with maximal effectiveness. Unexpected reserve powers come forth when the demand is strong enough. With growing interest, attention grows, and we are enabled to accomplish more.

15. The sources of interest, which are the approaches to attention, are many. Each sense-organ is a gateway to the mind of the pupil. Infants are lured by a bit of bright ribbon, and will cease crying to gaze upon some strange object swung before their eyes. The orator's gesturing hand, his smiling or passionate look, his many-toned voice often do more to hold the attention of his auditors than the meaning of his speech. The mind attends to that which makes a powerful appeal to the senses.

Sources of Interest

16. The teacher may not have the orator's opportunity for free gesticulation and commanding use of the voice; but within narrower limits he has it in his power to use face, voice, and hand. A sudden pause, with lifted hand, will arrest confusion and cause the pupils to listen and give attention. The showing of a picture, or of some other illustrative material, will attract the most careless and awaken the most apathetic. The sudden raising or lowering of the voice arouses fresh attention. All of these have value.

17. But let it be remembered that these are only devices to be employed when necessary; your effort at all times should be to make your presentation so interesting that the attention of the pupils will follow it. Teach the pupils to concentrate; they will soon pass through the stage of *active attention* and reach the effective stage of *secondary passive attention.* Resort to artificial stimuli only as a last means to gain attention.

18. A source of genuine interest may be found in the relation of the lesson to something in the past life of the learner, and a still richer one in the relation of the lesson to his future. We may add to these the sympathetic interest inspired by the teacher's delight in the theme, and by the emulation of the pupil's fellow learners in the same field. All these touch the pupil's personality, for an appeal is made to enlightened self-interest.

Interest Varies with Age

19. The sources of interest vary with the ages of the learners, with the advancing stages of growth and intelligence. This fact is important. The child of six, in general, feels no interest in and gives no attention to many themes which attract the youth of sixteen. Children and adults are often interested in the same scenes and objects, but usually not in the same phases of them. The child finds some striking fact of sense or some personal gratification an adequate stimulus to attention; the adult attends to the profounder relations, to the causes or the consequences. As children approach maturity, their interests tend to change from the concrete and more self-centered things to the abstract and ultimate.

20. Since attention follows interest, it is folly to attempt to gain attention without first stimulating interest. It is true that it is the duty of children to pay attention to the performance of their lessons; but the sense of duty must be felt by the child as well as by the teacher. In the very little child, this sense of duty may be represented in part by affection and sympathy, and through these he may be made to feel the claims of obligations which he cannot as yet fully understand. The little pupil may thus be led to feel an interest in things which the teacher loves and praises, before he has come fully to comprehend their importance.

21. The power of attention increases with the mental development, and is proportioned to the years of the child. Very short lessons will exhaust the attention of little children. "Little and often" should be the rule for teaching these little people. Prolonged attention belongs to more mature minds.

Hindrances to Attention

22. The two chief hindrances to attention are apathy and distraction. The former may be due to a lack of taste for the subject under consideration, or to weariness or some other physical condition. Distraction is the division of the attention among several objects, and is the foe of all learning. If the apathy or distraction comes from fatigue or illness, the wise teacher will not attempt to force the lesson.

Rules for Teachers

23. Out of this Law of the Learner emerge some of the most important rules of teaching:

(1) Never begin a class exercise until the attention of the class has been secured. Study for a moment the faces of the pupils to see if all are mentally, as well as bodily, present.

(2) Pause whenever the attention is interrupted or lost, and wait until it is completely regained.

(3) Never wholly exhaust the attention of your pupils. Stop as soon as signs of fatigue appear.

(4) Adapt the length of the class exercise to the ages of the pupils: the younger the pupils, the briefer the lesson.

(5) Arouse attention when necessary by variety in your presentation, but be careful to avoid distractions; keep the real lesson in view.

(6) Kindle and maintain the highest possible interest in the subject. Interest and attention react upon each other.

(7) Present those aspects of the lesson, and use such illustrations as will correspond to the ages and attainments of the pupils.

(8) Appeal whenever possible to the interests of your pupils.

(9) The favorite stories, songs, and subjects of the pupils are often keys to their interest and attention. Find out what these are, and make use of them.

(10) Look for sources of distraction, such as unusual noises, inside the classroom and out, and reduce them to a minimum.

(11) Prepare *beforehand* thought-provoking questions. Be sure that these are not beyond the ages and attainments of your pupils.

(12) Make your presentation as attractive as possible, using illustrations and all legitimate devices. Do not, however, let these devices be so prominent as themselves to become sources of distraction.

(13) Maintain and exhibit in yourself the closest attention to and most genuine interest in the lesson. True enthusiasm is contagious.

(14) Study the best use of the eye and the hand. Your pupils will respond to your earnest gaze and your lifted hand.

24. The violations of the Law of the Learner are

Violations and Mistakes

numerous and they constitute the most serious errors of many teachers.

(1) Recitations are commenced before the attention of the pupils has been gained, and continued after it has ceased to be given. One might as well begin before the pupils have entered the room, or continue after they have left.

(2) Pupils are urged to listen after their power of attention has been exhausted, and when fatigue has set in.

(3) Little or no effort is made to discover the tastes or experiences of the pupils, or to create a real interest in the subject. The teacher, himself feeling no great interest in his work, seeks to compel the attention which he is unable to attract, and awakens disgust instead of delight.

(4) Not a few teachers kill the power of attention in their pupils by failing to utilize any fresh inquiries or any new, interesting statements to stimulate interest in the subject. They drone on through their work, thinking of it themselves as routine. Naturally the pupils soon assume the same attitude.

25. What wonder that through these and other violations of this law of teaching our schoolrooms are often unattractive and their success so limited! And if obedience to these rules is so important in the public schools, where the attendance of children is compelled, and where the professional instructor teaches with full authority of the law, it is all the more necessary in the Sunday school, where attendance and teaching are voluntary. The Sunday school teacher who would win the richest and best results of teaching should give to this Law of the Learner his best thought and most thorough obedience. He should master the art of gaining and keeping attention, and of exciting genuine interest, and he will rejoice at the fruitfulness of his work.

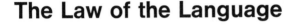

The Law of the Language

1. We have now, confronting each other, the teacher with his law of knowledge, and the learner with his condition of interested attention. We are next to study the medium of communication between them and learn the Law of the Language.

2. Two persons, who have material bodies which are limiting prisons, are to be brought into intellectual intercourse—the fine commerce of thought and feeling. There are no known spiritual connections between individuals in this world. Here the organs of sense are parts of material bodies, and can be touched and impressed only by matter and material phenomena. Out of these phenomena persons must construct the symbols and signs by which they can signal to one another the ideas which they wish to communicate. A system of such symbols or signs is a language. It may consist of the picture writing of the savage races, the alphabet systems of civilized peoples, the manual signs of the deaf-mutes, the oral speech of the hearing; but, whatever its form, it is language— a medium of communication between minds, a necessary instrument of teaching, and having, like all other factors in the teaching art, its own law.

3. This law, like those already discussed, is as simple as an everyday fact. It may be stated as follows: *The language used in teaching must be common to teacher and learner.* In other words, it must be understood by each, with the same meaning to both.

The Philosophy of the Law

4. The Law of the Language reaches down into the deepest facts of mind, and runs out to the widest connections of thought with life and with the world in which we live. The power of thought rests largely upon this fabric of speech.

5. Language in its simplest form is a system of artificial signs. Its separate words or signs may have no likeness to the things they signify, and no meanings except those that we give to them arbitrarily. A word is the sign of an idea only to the one who has the idea and who has learned the word as its sign or symbol. Without the image or the idea in the mind, the word comes to the ear only as a sound without meaning, a sign of nothing at all. No one has more language than he has learned. The vocabulary of the teacher may be many times larger than that of the pupil, but the child's ideas are represented by his vocabulary, and the teacher must come within this sphere of the child's language power if he would be understood. Outside of these limits, the language of the teacher will be characterized by lack of meaning, or perhaps perverted meaning, in proportion as the unfamiliar words exceed the familiar ones.

6. Many words in our language have more than one meaning. For example, consider the following expressions: *mind and matter; what is the matter? what matters it? it is a serious matter; the subject matter . . .* ; the same word is made to carry several meanings. This variety of meanings may enrich words for the use of the orator or the poet, but it presents difficulty for the young learner. Having mastered a word as the sign of a familiar idea, he is suddenly confronted by it with a new and unknown meaning. He has learned, perhaps, to tie a horse to a post, when he hears the strange text, *"My days are swifter than a post,"* or reads the warning, *"Post no bills,"* and hears of a *"military post."* The teacher, knowing all the meanings of his words, and guided by the context in selecting the one required by the thought, reads on or talks on, thinking perhaps that his language is rich in ideas and bright with meaning; but his pupils, knowing perhaps only a single meaning for each word, are stopped by great gaps in the sense, bridged only by sounds without meaning which puzzle and confuse them. It would often amuse us if we could know what ideas our words call up in little children. The boy who wanted to see "the wicked *flea* whom no man pursueth," and the other who said, "Don't view me with a *cricket's* eye," have many companions in the schools.

The Vehicle of Thought

7. Language has been called the *vehicle* of thought; but it does not carry thoughts as trucks carry goods, to fill an empty storehouse. Rather it conveys them as the wires convey telegrams, as signals to the receiving operator, who must re-translate the messages from the ticks he hears. Not what the speaker expresses from his own mind, but what the hearer understands and reproduces in *his* mind, measures the communicating power of the language used. Words that are poor and weak to the young and untrained may be eloquent with many rich and impressive meanings to the mature, trained mind. Thus the simple word *art* may mean "craft" to some minds, a mechanic's "trade," or even the pretense of a hypocrite; to a Reynolds or a Ruskin it is also the expression of all that is beautiful in human achievement, and of all that is elevating in civilization. It speaks of paintings, sculpture and cathedrals, and of all that is beautiful in nature, in landscape, sky, and sea—all that is noble or picturesque in history and life—all that is hidden in the moral and aesthetic nature of man. Men's words are like ships laden with the riches of every shore of knowledge which their owner has visited; while the words of the child are but toy boats on which are loaded the simple notions he has picked up in his brief experience.

8. So, too, words often come to be liked or disliked for the ideas they suggest. Thus the word *religion* to many is sublime with the divinest and most profound meanings. It paints on the dark background of human history, filled with sin and sorrow, all that is glorious in the character and government of God, all that is highest in faith and feeling, and all that is hopeful and bright in the future of man. To the more worldly, religion is sometimes the name of a mass of more or less disagreeable ceremonies or of distasteful duties. To the atheist it suggests superstition and creeds. In some degree, such variations of meaning belong to hundreds of the common words of our language. That teacher will do the best work who chooses his words wisely, raising the most and the clearest images in the minds of his pupils.

9. The reason goes further. In all effective teaching, thought passes in two directions—from pupil to teacher as well as from teacher to pupil. It is as necessary for the teacher fully to understand the child, as for the child to understand the teacher. Oftentimes a pupil will load ordinary words with some strange, false, or distorted meanings, and the mistakes may remain uncorrected for years. Children are often compelled by their very poverty of speech to use words with other than their correct meanings. The teacher must learn the needs of the pupil from his words.

10. But language is the *instrument,* as well as

The Instrument of Thought

the vehicle of thought. Words are tools under the plastic touch of which the mind reduces the crude mass of its impressions into clear and valid conceptions. Ideas become incarnate in words; they take form in language, and stand ready to be studied and known, to be marshaled into the mechanism of intelligible thought. Until they are thus given expression, they are like vague phantoms, indistinct and intangible. It is one of the most important functions of teaching to help the child to gain a full and clear expression of what he already knows imperfectly. No teaching is complete that does not issue in plain and intelligent expression of the lesson; this means that the expression should be in the language of the child, and not mere repetition of ready-made definitions of someone else, in words very likely in many cases to be totally unfamiliar.

11. We may go even further and say that talking is thinking, for ideas must precede words in all but parrot speech. The most useful, and sometimes the most difficult processes in thinking are those in which we fit words to ideas. The full and clear statement of a problem is often the best part of solving it. Ideas rise before us at first like the confused mass of objects in a new landscape; to put them into clear and correct words and sentences is to make the landscape familiar.

Thoughts disentangle passing o'er the lip.

12. We master truth by expressing it, and are

glad when we have clearly expressed our thought. But in order to make *talking* into *thinking,* there must be independent and original effort, not a mere parrotlike repetition of the words of other people. The pupil himself must do much of the talking. What teacher has not watched the battle when a little group of children have attacked some knotty problem, and each has tried to reduce the truth to proper speech? and how proud the victor when he has forced the thought into fitting words which all recognized as the true expression! Krusi[1] tells of one of his pupils who was told to write a letter to his parents, and complained: "It is hard for me to write a letter." "Why! you are now a year older, and ought to be better able to do it." "Yes, but a year ago I could say everything I knew, but now I know more than I can say." Krusi adds: "This answer astonished me." It will surprise all of us who have not thought of the difficulty of obtaining sufficient mastery of language to express our thoughts.

13. Language has still another use; it is the *storehouse* of our knowledge. All that we know may be found laid up in the words concerning it. Thus words are not only the signs of our ideas, but they are clues by which we recover and recognize those ideas at will, and in the manifold derivative forms and combinations of these

---

[1] Hermann Krusi was a friend and fellow-worker of the great Swiss schoolmaster and educational reformer, Pestalozzi (1746-1827).

words, we store up the modifications and relations of the notion of which the simple word is the symbol. A group of words like act, acted, acting, actor, actress, action, actionable, active, actively, actual, actually, actualize, actuality, actuate, suggests a large volume of facts concerning persons, movements, relations, qualities, etc.

14. The language of the child, then, may be considered not only the measure of his attainments, but the embodiment of the elements of his knowledge. When we employ in our teaching the language of our pupils, we summon to our aid their acquired experience. New words must be learned when new objects are to be named or new ideas are to be symbolized; but if care is taken that the idea shall go before the word and that the word is mastered as a symbol before it is used in speech, it will guide and illumine rather than cloud the child's perception.

The Language of Objects

15. Words are not the only medium through which to speak. There are many ways to express thought. The eye, the head, the hand, the foot, the shoulder, are often used in speech in ways that are most intelligible. Among savage peoples whose language is too meager to meet their needs, symbolic actions often take the place of words. The gestures of some speakers frequently tell more than the spoken sentences of others. There is speech also in pictures. From rough sketches on the blackboard to paintings that are works of art, teaching by pictorial representation is swift and impressive.

16. Finally, nature aids speech.

> . . . she speaks a various language.

Her innumerable forms are always ready as effective illustrations, and her analogies throw light on many deep problems. No teaching was ever more instructive than the parables of Jesus, drawn from nature around Him.

17. Ordinary artificial language probably must be the chief means of communication between teacher and pupil; but no wise teacher will forego the aid of all these various means of entrance to the minds of their pupils. Language by itself is at best but an imperfect medium of thought, and no one knows this better than the experienced teacher, who has sometimes found it ineffective, and who has been compelled to resort to any available means of illustration to make himself understood.

18. This discussion of language should not be interpreted as an encouragement to the teacher to become a lecturer before his class. The lecture is useful in its place, but its place is. small in a school for children. It will be shown elsewhere that a too talkative teacher is rarely a good teacher. An accurate knowledge of language is, however, of great advantage; those who talk little should certainly talk well, and those who expect to teach through language should know language themselves.

Rules for Teachers

19. Out of our Law of Languages, thus defined and explained, flow some of the most useful rules for teaching.

(1) Study constantly and carefully the language of the pupils, to learn what words they use and what meanings they give to these words.

(2) Secure from them as full a statement as possible of their knowledge of the subject, to learn both their ideas and their modes of expressing them, and to help them to correct their knowledge.

(3) Express yourself as far as possible in the language of your pupils, carefully correcting any errors in the meaning they read into your words.

(4) Use the simplest and the fewest words that will express your meaning. Unnecessary words add to the child's work, and increase the possibilities for misunderstanding.

(5) Use short sentences, of the simplest construction. Long sentences are difficult to attend to and are frequently confusing to children.

(6) If the pupil obviously fails to understand you, repeat your thought in other language, if possible with greater simplicity.

(7) Help the meaning of the words by illustrations; natural objects and pictures are to be preferred for young children. Take illustrations

from the children's own experiences whenever possible.

(8) When it is necessary to teach a new word, give the idea before the word. This can be done best by simple illustrations closely related to the children's own experience.

(9) Try to increase the number of the pupil's words, and at the same time improve the clearness of meaning. Real enlargement of a child's vocabulary means an increase of his knowledge and power.

(10) As the acquisition of language is one of the important aims in the process of education, do not be content to have your pupils listen in silence very long at a time, no matter how attentive they are. Encourage them to talk freely.

(11) Here, as everywhere in teaching the young, *make haste slowly.* Each word should be learned thoroughly before others are added.

(12) Test frequently the pupil's understanding of the words that he uses, to make sure that he attaches no incorrect meaning and that he sees the true meaning as vividly as possible.

20. This third law of teaching is violated more frequently than the best teachers suspect.

Violations and Mistakes

(1) The interested look of the pupils often cheats the teacher into the belief that his language is thoroughly understood, and all the more easily because the pupil himself may be deceived and say that he understands, when he has per-

haps caught only a mere glimpse of the meaning.

(2) Children are often entertained by the manner of the teacher, and seem attentive to his words when really they are watching only his eyes, lips, or actions. Again, they will sometimes profess to understand simply to please their instructor and gain his praise.

(3) The misuse of language is one of the common faults in teaching. Not to mention those teachers who attempt to cover up their own ignorance or indolence with a cloud of verbiage which they know the children will not understand, and omitting also those who are more anxious to exhibit their own wisdom than to teach others, there are still many honest teachers who try hard to make the lesson clear, and then think that their duty is done; that if the children do not understand, it must be either from wilful inattention or hopeless stupidity. These teachers do not suspect that they may have used words which had no meaning for the class, or into which the children read a wrong meaning.

(4) It may be a single unusual or misunderstood term that breaks the connection, but it does not occur to the teacher to hunt up the break and restore the connection. Children do not always ask for explanations, discouraged sometimes by fear of the teacher, or shame for their own ignorance, and too often they are charged with stupidity or inattention when no amount of attention

would have helped them to understand the unfamiliar language.

(5) Even those teachers who naturally use simple language to their classes sometimes fail in the higher uses of this instrument of teaching. They do not take the trouble to secure from the child in return some clear statement, and they have, therefore, no test of their success. The children do not talk themselves, nor are their vocabularies enlarged.

(6) Many teachers have no proper appreciation of the wonderful character and complexity of language; they do not reflect that modern society could scarcely exist without speech. Many persons have decidedly limited vocabularies. It has often been found that one of the greatest obstacles to the general enlightenment of people lies in their lack of the knowledge through which they must be addressed. A commission from the British Parliament was once sent to investigate the language of the coal miners and other laborers of England in order to ascertain the possibility of diffusing useful information among them by means of tracts and books. It was found that their knowledge of language, in a large number of the cases examined, was entirely too meager to permit of such a means of instruction. How much greater this deficiency must be among the young, whose experience is so much more limited. If we would teach children successfully, we must widen and

deepen this channel of communication between them and ourselves.

(7) Many of the topics studied in school lie outside the daily life and language of the children; and every science has a language of its own which must be mastered by the student who makes any progress in it. The teacher in the Sunday school should recognize that here lies one of his problems; many times the facts and truths of religion are likely to be distorted by the half-understood terms in which they are told. To the teacher of children in the schools of Bible learning should come the warning to make his words clear.

The Law of the Lesson

1. Our fourth law takes us at once to the core of teaching. The first three laws dealt with the teacher, the learner, and the language, the medium of communication between them. We come now to the lesson, the process to be mastered, the problem to be solved. This is where the teacher must pass on to the pupils the recorded experience of the race; the method of transmission of this crystallized race experience must be such as to inspire these pupils with principles that shall be active forces in their lives, and at the same time furnish them with an instrument of research and further study—this is the very heart of the work of the teacher, the condition and instrument, as well as the culmination and the fruit, of all the rest.

2. It is the Law of the Lesson that we are next to seek. Passing, as remote from this discussion, the steps by which the mind of an infant obtains its first notions of the world about it, we may go at once to the obvious fact that our pupils learn the new by the aid of the old and familiar. The new and unknown can be explained only by the familiar and the known. This, then, is the Law of the Lesson: *The truth to be taught must be learned through truth already known.*

3. This law is neither so simple nor so obvious as those that have preceded it; but it is no less certain than they, while its scope is even wider and its relations are perhaps even more important.

The Philosophy of the Law

4. The Law of the Lesson has its reason in the nature of mind and in the nature of human knowledge.

5. All teaching must begin at some point of the subject or lesson. If the subject is wholly new, then a known point must be sought by showing some likeness of the new to something known and familiar. Even among grown persons, the skilful narrator struggles to find some comparison with familiar experiences, seeking some likeness of the unknown to something known before proceeding with his story. Until this starting point is found, he knows that it will be useless to go on. To do so would be like telling someone to follow you over a winding path in the darkness without first letting him know where you are or starting him on the path. Naturally, if adults must have this aid, children can scarcely be expected to do without it. Often pupils in the schools explain their inability to understand the lesson by the simple statement:

"I did not know what the teacher was talking about." The fault lies distinctly with the teacher in such a case.

6. All teaching must advance in some direction. Its proper direction of march should be toward the acquisition of new experiences. To teach over again what is already acquired and understood is to check the desire of the pupils for obtaining further knowledge and to deaden their power of attention by compelling them to walk in a treadmill, instead of leading them forward to the inspiration of new scenes and the conquest of new fields. It is a serious error to keep the studies of pupils too long on familiar ground under the assumed necessity for thoroughness. Old mines may be reworked if you can find ore at deeper levels, and old lessons may be worked over if new uses may be made of them. At this point it should be borne in mind that this does not contradict the Law of Review, to be discussed later.

7. Learning must proceed by graded steps. These steps must be those which link one fact or concept to another, as simple and concrete things lead naturally to general and abstract things, as premises lead to conclusions, and as an understanding of natural phenomena leads to laws. Each new idea mastered becomes a part of the knowledge of the child, a part of his equipment of race experience, and serves as a starting point for a fresh advance. It adds its own light to the knowledge that preceded it, and throws increased illumination forward for the next discovery. But each step must be fully mastered before the next is taken, or the pupils may find themselves proceeding into unknown fields without the proper preparation. It is here that the demand for thoroughness arises; everything in the lesson which is within the range of the child's comprehension, should be fully understood. Thoroughness of this sort is the essential condition of true teaching. Imperfect understanding at any point clouds the whole process. The pupil who has mastered one lesson, half knows the next; therefore the well-taught class is always eager for the next step. One of the sayings of Pestalozzi was: "It is easy to add to what is already discovered."

8. But the philosophy of this law goes deeper still. It must be remembered that knowledge is not a mass of simple, independent facts; it is made up of the experience of the race crystallized and *organized* in the form of facts together with their laws and relations. Facts are linked together in systems, associated by resemblances of one sort or another. Each fact leads to, and explains, another. The old reveals the new; the new confirms and corrects the old.

9. All this pertains equally to the limited knowledge and experience of children as well as to riper and maturer knowledge. New elements of knowledge must be brought into relation with other facts and truths already known before they themselves can be fully revealed and take their place in the widening circle of the experience of the learner. Thus the very nature of knowledge compels us to seek the new through the aid of the old.

10. The act of *knowing* is in part an act of comparing and judging—of finding something in past experience that will explain and make meaningful the new experience. If a friend tells us of an experience or an adventure, we interpret his story by a running comparison with whatever has been most like it in our own experience; and if he states something utterly without likeness to anything that we have known, we ask him for explanations or illustrations which may bring the strange facts into relation with our point of view. If children are told something novel and entirely unfamiliar, they will probably struggle in vain to understand, and then ask for further information or light, if they do not at once abandon the attempt to connect the new idea with their own experience. Figures of speech, such as similes, metaphors, and allegories, have sprung out of the need for relating new truths to old and familiar scenes and objects and experiences. They are but so many attempts to reach the unknown through the known—they try to flash light from the old upon the new.

11. Explanation, then, means usually the citation

and use of fact and principles already understood to make clear the nature of new material. Therefore the unknown cannot explain the unknown. The knowledge already in the equipment of the child must furnish the explanation of new facts and laws, or these must remain unexplained. The difficulty so often met in answering the questions of little children, lies not so much in the difficulty of the questions themselves, as in the lack upon the part of the child of knowledge required in the explanation. To answer fully a boy's questions about the stars, you must first teach him some astronomy. The lad who has seen a large city can perhaps understand fairly well a description of London or New York, but one whose experience has been confined entirely to his country home, cannot properly understand the network of streets, walled in by buildings, and the shifting panorama of city life.

12. The very language with which new knowledge must be expressed takes its meanings from what is already known and familiar. The child without knowledge would be also without words, for words are the signs of things known. An American traveler in Europe might perhaps fancy that he could make people understand by speaking in a loud, clear voice, and with slow, careful enunciation; but his success would be measured only by the degree to which his hearers had a knowledge of the native tongue of the American; if they were foreigners, familiar only with their own language, his words would be without meaning.

13. A blunder analogous to this is that of the teacher who hopes by the mere urgency of his manner, and by his carefully chosen words, familiar to himself, to convey his ideas to the understanding of his pupils, with no reference to the pupils' previous knowledge of the subject.

14. Persons use by preference only the clearest and most familiar things in their interpretation of new facts or principles. Each man is prone to borrow his illustrations from his calling: the soldier from the camps and trenches, the sailor from the ships and the sea, the merchant from the conditions of the market, and the artisans and mechanics from their crafts. Likewise in study, each pupil is attracted to the qualities which relate to his own experience. To the chemist, common salt is sodium chloride, a binary compound; to the cook it is something to use in the seasoning of foods and in the preservation of meats. Each thinks of it in the aspect most familiar to him, and in this aspect would use it to illustrate something else in which salt was concerned. Finding a new plant, the botanist would consider it in the light of known plants, to discover its "classification"; the farmer would be interested in its use, and the artist in its beauty. This bent of preference, while one of the elements of prejudice which may shut the eyes to some new truths and open them to others, is at the same time one of the elements of strength in intellectual work.

15. A fact or principle only vaguely understood is used only rarely and reluctantly—and even then sometimes most erroneously—in interpreting new experiences; and if used, it carries only vagueness and imperfection into the new concepts or judgments. A cloud left upon the lesson of yesterday casts its shadow over the lesson of today. On the other hand, the thoroughly mastered lesson throws great light on the succeeding ones. Hence the value of that practice of some able teachers who make the elementary portions of a subject as familiar as household words—a conquered territory from which the pupil may go on to new conquests as from an established base, with confidence and power.

16. But it must be carefully noted that so complete a mastery, like all thoroughness in study, is really relative. No human knowledge or power is perfect and the capacities of childhood are necessarily much further from completeness than those of adults. And there are wide individual differences which must be recognized in the school. What to some children is as clear as day, is to others only vaguely suggestive. If the teacher makes the pupils talk about the lesson, as was suggested in the discussion of the law of language, some of these differences will be revealed, and the proper means of meeting them and of adjusting the instruction to them, may be discovered.

17. Our discussion of the lesson would be incomplete without some mention of the nature of the thinking process as applied to the solution of problems. The word "problem" is a familiar one to the teacher; the problems and tasks of everyday life in the schoolroom are very close to him. But let us now think of the problem in a rather different sense. We have been speaking of the "lesson" and its "law." Let us think of the process of learning lessons as akin to the solution of problems, as a process in which the learner faces a real situation, the mastery of which will involve the application of his power of thought. How is he to think?

18. The older notion that because the pupils in our schools are young and immature they are incapable of real thinking is a fallacy. Too often teachers believe that their pupils think only in a symbolic way—that they react only to artificial situations in which their task is to do what the teacher wishes, rather than to do real independent thinking for themselves. This is not necessarily true, and if true in some instances, the fault very likely lies with the teacher himself. The fact is that the power to think is part and parcel of the original mental equipment of the child, and develops gradually, as other capacities do. The situations that call out this power in children are simple, but they are none the less real. The difference in thinking between the child and the adult is a difference in degree.

19. If we are to set the learner at the task of real thinking in the solution of real problems, we must define this process of thinking. There are three stages in the process. First, there must be a stage of doubt or uncertainty; certain things are known, and something is to be done to them. For example, the loss of a cherished toy presents just this situation to a child: he sees what has happened, and wonders what he can do in its absence—how he can replace it, perhaps. Second, there is an organizing stage in which the individual considers the means at his disposal to reach the ends desired. Lastly, there is a critical attitude involving selection and rejection of the schemes which have suggested themselves. This problematic situation arises very frequently in daily life, with children as well as with adults. The setting of school tasks should always be done with this process of thinking in mind; teachers in the day schools and in the Sunday schools should remember that if the training which they give is to bear fruit, it must present real situations which will call forth this reflective attitude, and they should abjure the sort of tasks which can be met by trial and error, by blindly following the lead of another, or by doing what one has already done in a similar situation merely because one recognizes the new situation as like the other.

20. In a very important sense, what we call knowledge is a record of solved problems. Facts and laws have been collected and tested and organized into systems, but at basis they represent the results of facing situations and finding things out at first hand. In passing knowledge on to others the more closely we can approximate real, vital situations, the better will be our teaching. There are some who go so far as to say that no attempt should be made to impart knowledge unless the child feels a distinct need for it—unless he sees that it is essential to solve some problem that is real and vital to his life. This is doubtless an extreme view, but it is none the less incumbent upon the teacher to know what the problems of child life are and to utilize them in making his instruction just as rich and meaningful as possible.

Rules for Teachers

21. This law of knowledge, thus explained, affords to the thoughtful teacher rules of the highest practical value. It offers clear guidance to those who are teachers of children and anxious that their task shall be well done.

(1) Find out what your pupils know of the subject you wish to teach to them; this is your starting point. This refers not only to textbook

knowledge but to all information that they may possess, however acquired.

(2) Make the most of the pupils' knowledge and experience. Let them feel its extent and value, as a means to further knowledge.

(3) Encourage your pupils to clear up and freshen their knowledge by a clear statement of it.

(4) Begin with facts or ideas that lie near your pupils, and that can be reached by a single step from what is already familiar; thus, geography naturally begins with the home town, history with the pupils' own memories, morals with their own conscience.

(5) Relate every lesson as much as possible to former lessons, and with the pupils' knowledge and experience.

(6) Arrange your presentation so that each step of the lesson shall lead easily and naturally to the next.

(7) Proportion the steps of the lesson to the ages and attainments of your pupils. Do not discourage your children with lessons or exercises that are too long, or fail to rise to the expectations of older pupils by giving them lessons that are too easy.

(8) Find illustrations in the commonest and most familiar objects suitable for the purpose.

(9) Lead the pupils themselves to find illustrations from their own experience.

(10) Make every new fact or principle fa-

miliar to your pupils; try to establish and intrench it firmly, so that it will be available for use in explaining new material to come.

(11) Urge the pupils to make use of their own knowledge and attainments in every way that is practicable, to find or explain other knowledge. Teach them that knowledge is power by showing how knowledge really helps to solve problems.

(12) Make every advance clear and familiar, so that the progress to the next succeeding step shall in every case be on known ground.

(13) As far as possible, choose the problems which you give to your pupils from their own activities, and thus increase the chances that they will be real and not artificial problems.

(14) Remember that your pupils are learning to think, and that to think properly they must learn to face intelligently and reflectively the problems that arise in connection with their school work, and in connection with their life outside of school.

22. The wide scope of this Law of the Lesson affords opportunity for many mistakes and violations. Among the more common are the following:

Mistakes and Violations

(1) It is not unusual for teachers to set their pupils to studying new lessons, or even new subjects, for which they are inadequately prepared or not prepared at all, either by previous study or by experience.

(2) Many teachers neglect entirely to ascertain carefully the pupils' equipment with which to begin the subject.

(3) A common error is the failure to connect the new lessons with those that have gone before in such a way that the pupils can carry over what they know or have learned into the new field. Many individual lessons and recitations are treated as if each were independent of all the others.

(4) Oftentimes past acquisitions are considered goods stored away, instead of instruments for further use.

(5) Too often elementary facts and definitions are not made thoroughly familiar.

(6) Every step is not always thoroughly understood before the next is attempted.

(7) Some teachers err in assigning lessons or exercises that are too long for the powers of the pupils, or for their time, making impossible an adequate mastery of principles that may be needful for future progress in the subject.

(8) Teachers frequently fail to place their pupils in the attitude of discoverers. Children should learn to use what they have already been taught in the discovery of new problems.

(9) A common fault is the failure to show the connections between parts of the subject that have been taught and those that are yet to come.

23. As a consequence of these and other violations of the law, much teaching is poor, and its benefits, if any, are fleeting. People are found to have inadequate knowledge and to lack the power of studying for themselves. This is as true of Biblical knowledge as of any other. Instead of a related whole, a concept with one purpose, the Bible is viewed as scattering parts, like bits of broken glass, and its effect is many times only to puzzle and confuse; it is never seen as a connected whole, as it should be.

The Law of the Teaching Process

1. Our survey of the teaching art has thus far involved these four considerations: the teacher, the learner, the language, and the lesson. We are now to study these in action, and to observe the conduct of the teacher and his pupil. The previous discussions have already brought these partly into view, but as each of them ·has its own law, each demands more careful consideration than has yet been given it. In the laws of the teacher and the learner, we found neoessarily reflected the actions of both; but an actor and his part are easily separated in thought, and each possesses aspects and characteristics of its own. Following the natural order, the teaching function comes first before us, and we are now to seek its law. The law of the teacher was essentially a law of qualification; the law of teaching is a law of function.

2. Thus far we have considered teaching as the communication of knowledge or experience; more properly, we should say that this is a *result* of teaching. Whether by telling, demonstrating, or leading pupils to discover for themselves, the teacher is transmitting experience to his pupils; that is his aim and purpose, and his teaching is conditioned by that aim. But the explanation of the work of the teacher in terms of function is to be distinguished from the definition in terms of purpose. The actual work of the teacher consists of the awakening and setting in action the mind of the pupil, the arousing of his self-activities. As already shown, knowledge cannot be passed from mind to mind like objects from one receptacle to another, but must in every case be recognized and rethought and relived by the receiving mind. All explanation and exposition are useless except as they serve to excite and direct the pupil in his own thinking. If the pupil himself does not think, there are no results of the teaching; the words of the teacher are falling upon deaf ears.

The Law of Teaching

3. We are now ready to state the law of teaching: *Excite and direct the self-activities of the pupil, and as a rule tell him nothing that he can learn himself.*

4. The second clause in this law is of sufficient importance to justify its position in the formulation of the law, although it is negatively stated. There are cases in which it may be necessary to disregard this caution in order to save time, or in the case of a very weak or discouraged pupil, or sometimes when intense interest has been aroused and there is a keen demand for information that the teacher can give quickly and effectively, but its violation is almost always a loss which should be compensated by a definite gain. Considered affirmatively, this caution would read: "Make your pupil a discoverer of truth—make him find out for himself." The great value of this law has been so often and so strongly stated as to demand no further proof. No great writer on education has failed to consider it in some form or another; if we were seeking the educational maxim most widely received among good teachers, and the most extensive in its applications and results, we should fix upon this law. It is the same fundamental truth as the one found in such rules as the following: "Wake up your pupils' minds"; "Set the pupils to thinking"; "Arouse the spirit of inquiry"; "Get your pupils to work." All these familiar maxims are different expressions of this same law.

5. In discussing the principles of attention, language, and knowledge, we have considered to some extent the operations of the mind. We should now study these further.

6. We can learn without a teacher. Children learn hundreds of facts before they ever see a school, sometimes with the aid of parents or others, often by their own unaided efforts. In the greater part

The Philosophy of the Law

of our acquisitions we are self-taught, and it is quite generally conceded that that knowledge is most permanent and best which is dug out by unaided research. Everything, at the outset, must be learned by the discoverer without an instructor, since no instructor knows it. If, then, we can learn without being taught, it follows that the true function of the teacher is to create the most favorable conditions for self-learning. Essentially the acquisition of knowledge must be brought about by the same agencies and through the use of the same methods, whether with or without a teacher.

7. What, then, is the use of schools, and what is the necessity of a teacher? The question is pertinent, but the answer is plain. Knowledge in its natural state lies scattered and confused; it is connected, to be sure, in great systems, but these connections are laws and relations unknown to the beginner, and they are to be learned by man only through ages of observation and careful study. The school selects for its curriculum what it regards as the most useful of the experiences of the race, organizes these, and offers them to the pupils along with its facilities for learning. It offers to these pupils leisure and quiet for study, and through its books and other materials of education the results of other people's labors, which may serve as charts of the territories to be explored, and as beaten paths through the fields of knowledge. True teaching, then, is not that which *gives* knowledge, but that which stimulates pupils to *gain* it. One might say that he teaches *best* who teaches *least;* or that he teaches best whose pupils learn most without being taught directly. But we should bear in mind that in these epigrammatic statements two meanings of the word *teaching* are involved,—one, simply telling, the other creating the conditions of real learning.

8. That teacher is a sympathizing guide whose knowledge of the subjects to be studied enables him properly to direct the efforts of the pupil, to save him from a waste of time and strength, from needless difficulties. But no aid of school or teacher can change the operations of the mind, or take from the pupil his need of knowing for himself. The eye must do its own seeing, the ear its own hearing, and the mind its own thinking, however much may be done to furnish objects of sights, sounds for the ear and stimuli for the intelligence. The innate capacities of the child produce the growth of body or mind. "If childhood is educated according to the measure of its powers," said Saint Augustine, "they will continually grow and increase; while if forced beyond their strength, they decrease instead of increasing." The sooner the teacher abandons the notion that he can make his pupils intelligent by hard work upon their passive receptivity, the sooner he will become a good teacher and obtain the art, as Socrates said, of assisting the mind to shape and put forth its own conceptions. It was to his skill in this that the great Athenian owed his power and greatness among his contemporaries, and it was this that gave him his place as one of the foremost of the great teachers of mankind. It is the "forcing process" in teaching which separates parrotlike and perfunctory *learning* from *knowing*. A boy, having expressed surprise at the shape of the earth when he was shown a globe, was asked: "Did you not learn that in school?" He repied: "Yes, I learned it, but I never knew it."

9. The great aims of education are to acquire knowledge and ideals, and to develop abilities and skills. Our law derives its significance from both of these aims. The pupil must know for himself, or his knowledge will be knowledge in name only. The very effort required in the act of thus learning and knowing may do much to increase the capacity to learn. The pupil who is taught without doing any studying for himself will be like one who is fed without being given any exercise: he will lose both his appetite and his strength.

10. Confidence in our own powers is an essential condition of their successful use. This confidence can be gained only by self-prompted, voluntary, and independent use of these capacities. We learn to walk, not by seeing others walk, but by walking. The same is true of mental abilities.

11. The self-activities or mental powers do not set themselves at work without some motive or stimulus to put them in action. In early life external stimuli are stronger, and in riper years the internal excitants are the ones to which we respond more readily. To the young child the objects of sense— bright colors, live animals, and things in motion— are most attractive and exciting. Later in life, the inner facts of thought and feeling are more engaging. The child's mental life has in it an excess of sensation; the mental life of the adult has more reflection.

12. But whatever the stimulus, the processes of cognition are largely the same. There is the comparison of the new with the old, the alternating analysis and synthesis of parts, wholes, classes, causes, and effects; the action of memory and imagination, the use of judgment and reason, and the effects upon thought of tastes and prejudices as they have been concerned with the previous knowledge and experience of the learner. If thinking does not take place, the teacher has applied the stimuli in vain. He perhaps will wonder that his pupils do not understand, and will very likely consider them stupid and incompetent, or at least lazy. Unfortunately the stupidity is sometimes on the other side, and it sins against this law of teaching in assuming that the teacher can *make* the pupil learn by dint of vigorous telling, or teaching as he calls it, whereas true teaching only brings to bear on the pupil's mind certain natural stimuli or excitants. If some of these fail, he must find others, and not rest until he attains the desired result and sees the activity of the child at work upon the lesson.

13. Comenius[1] said, over two hundred years ago, "Most teachers sow plants instead of seeds; instead of proceeding from the simplest principles they introduce the pupil at once into a chaos of books and miscellaneous studies." The figure of the seed is a good one, and is much older than Comenius. The greatest of teachers said: "The seed is the word." The true teacher stirs the ground and sows the seed. It is the work of the soil, through its own forces, to develop the growth and ripen the grain.

14. The difference between the pupil who works for himself and the one who works only when he is driven is too obvious to need explanation. The one is a free agent, the other is a machine. The former is attracted by his work, and, prompted by his interest, he works on until he meets some overwhelming difficulty or reaches the end of his

[1] Johann Amos Comenius (1592-1671) was a Moravian clergyman, whose efforts to reform school practices have given him an enduring place in the history of education.

task. The latter moves only when he is urged. He sees what is shown him, he hears what he is told, advances when his teacher leads, and stops just where and when the teacher stops. The one moves by his own activities, and the other by borrowed impulse. The former is a mountain stream fed by living springs, the latter a ditch filled from a pump worked by another's hand.

15. The action of the mind is limited practically to the field of its acquired knowledge. The individual who knows nothing cannot think, for he has nothing to think about. In comparing, imagining, judging, and reasoning, and in applying knowledge to plan, criticize, or execute one's own thoughts, the mind must necessarily work upon the material in its possession. Hence the power of any object or fact as a mental stimulus depends in each case upon the number of related objects or facts which the individual already knows. A botanist will be aroused to the keenest interest by the discovery of a hitherto unknown plant, but will perhaps care little or nothing for a new stone or a new star. The physician eagerly studies new diseases, the lawyer recent decisions, the farmer new crops, and the mechanic new machines.

Knowledge Necessary to Thought

16. The infant knows little, and his interest is brief and slight; the man knows many things, and his interests are deeper, wider, and more persistent. Thoughtfulness deepens and grows more intense with the increase of knowledge. The student of mathematics who has worked long and diligently in his field never finds it dry or tiresome; the wisest student of the Bible finds in its pages the greatest delight. All these illustrations show the principles which underlie our law and prove its value.

17. The two chief springs of interest through which the mind can be aroused are the love of knowledge for its own sake, that is, its cultural value, and the desire for knowledge to be used as a tool in solving problems or obtaining other knowledge. In the former are mingled the satisfaction of the native curiosity which craves to know the real nature and causes of the phenomena around us, the solution of the questionings which often trouble the mind, the relief from apprehensions which ignorance feels in the presence of nature's mysteries, the sense of power and liberty which knowledge often brings, the feeling of elevation which each new increment of knowledge gives, and the "rejoicing in the truth" because of its own beauty and sublimity, or its moral charm and sweetness, its appeals to our taste for wit and humor, and for the wonderful. All these enter separately or together into the intellectual appetite to which the various forms of knowledge appeal, and which give to reading and study their greatest attraction. Each affords an avenue through which the mind can be reached and roused by the skilful teacher.

18. It is evident that this manifold mental appetite must vary in character and intensity with the tastes and attainments of the pupils. Some love nature and her sciences of observation and experiment; others love mathematics and delight in its problems; still others prefer the languages and literature, and others history and the sciences which deal with the powers, deeds, and destinies of man. Each special preference grows by being fostered, and becomes absorbing as its acquisitions become great. The great masteries and achievements in arts, literature, and science have come from these innate tastes, and in all these "the child is father of the man."

In each pupil lies the germ of such tastes—the springs of such powers—awaiting the art of the teacher to water the germs and set the springs in motion.

19. The respect for knowledge because of its value as a tool includes the desire for education as a means of livelihood or as a source of better social standing; the felt or anticipated need of some special skill or ability as an artist, lawyer, writer, or some other brain worker; as well as study for the purpose of winning rewards or avoiding punishments. This indirect desire for learning varies with the character and aims of the pupils, but does not increase with attainment unless it ripens, as it may, into the true love of knowledge above described. Its strength depends upon the nature and magnitude of the need which impels the study. The activities aroused for such study go to a self-imposed task and are not very likely to continue their work after the task is done. The rewards and punishments used in school to promote the studying of lessons have just this force and no more. They inspire no generous activity which works for the love of the work and which does not pause when the assigned lesson has been covered. Witness the spirit that pervades every school so taught and so managed. On the other hand, if the true uses of knowledge are constantly pointed out by the teacher and recognized by the child, the time may well come when respect for knowledge because it is useful becomes a real love of knowledge for its own sake.

Knowledge and the Feelings

20. Our discussion thus far has taken for granted the intimate and indissoluble connection between the intellect and the feelings, the inseparable union of thought and feeling. To think without feeling would be thinking with a total indifference to the object of thought, which would be absurd; and to feel without thinking would be almost impossible. As most of the objects of thought are objects also of desire or dislike, and therefore objects of choice, it follows that all important action of the intellect has a moral side. This, again, is an assumption that we have made throughout our discussion. The love of knowledge for itself or for its uses is in reality moral, as it implies moral affections and purposes of good or evil. All motives of study have a moral character or connection, in their early steps; hence no education or teaching can be absolutely divorced from morals. The affections come to school with the intellect.

21. This moral consciousness finds its fuller sphere in the recognized domain of duty—the higher realm of the affections and the other moral qualities. From these come the highest and strongest incentives to study and also the clearest understanding. The teacher should constantly address the moral nature and stimulate moral sentiments, if he wishes to achieve the greatest measure of success.

22. This moral teaching was the chief merit of the work of Pestalozzi, and it is the leading characteristic of the work of all great teachers. Love of country, love of one's fellows, aspirations for a noble and useful life, love for truth—these are all motives to which appeal should be made. If these motives are lacking in pupils, the teacher must build them up.

23. It follows from all this that only when the mental powers work freely and in their own way can the product be sure or permanent. No one

The Self-Active Mind

can know exactly what any mind contains, or how it performs, save as that mind imperfectly reveals it by words or acts, or as we conceive it by reflecting upon our own conscious experience. Just as the disgestive organs must do their own work, masticating and digesting whatever food they receive, selecting, secreting, assimilating, and so building bone, muscle, nerve, and all the various tissues and organs of the body, so, too, in the last resort, the mind must perform its function, without external aid, building, as it can, concepts, faith, purposes, and all forms of intelligence and character. As Milton expressed it:—

> The mind is its own place, and in itself
> Can make a heaven of hell, a hell of heaven.

24. If the fact of the mind's autocracy is thus emphasized, it is not for the purpose of belittling the work of the teacher, but only to show more clearly the law which gives to that work all its force and dignity. It is the teacher's mission to stand at the spiritual gateways of his pupil's mind, serving as a herald of science, a guide through nature, to summon the minds to their work, to place before them the facts to be observed and studied, and to guide them into the right paths to be followed. It is his by sympathy, by example, and by every means of influence—by objects for the senses, by facts for the intelligence—to excite the mind of the pupils, to stimulate their thoughts.

25. The cautionary clause of our law which forbids giving too much help to pupils will be needless to the teacher who clearly sees his proper work. Like a skilful engineer who knows the power of his engine, he chooses to stand and watch the play of the splendid machine and marvel at the ease and vigor of its movements. It is only the unskilled teacher who prefers to hear his own voice in endless talk rather than to watch and direct the course of the thoughts of his pupils.

26. There is no disagreement beween this law and the first and third, which so strongly insist upon the teacher's knowledge of the subject. Without full and accurate knowledge of the subject that the pupil is to learn through his self-active efforts, the teacher certainly cannot guide, direct, and test the process of learning. One may as well say that a general need know nothing of a battlefield because he is not to do the actual fighting, as that a teacher may get on with inadequate knowledge because the pupils must do the studying. As we have said, there are exceptions to the rule that the pupil should be told nothing that he can discover for himself. There are some occasions when the teacher may, for a few moments, become a lecturer and, from his own more extensive experience, give his pupils broader, richer, and clearer views of the field of their work. But in such cases he must take care not to substitute mere telling for true teaching, and thus encourage passive listening where he needs to call for earnest work.

27. The most important stimuli used by nature to stir the minds of men have already been noted. They might all be described as the silent but ceaseless questions which the world and the universe are always addressing to man. The eternal questions of childhood are really the echoes of these greater questions. The object or the event that excites no question will provoke no thought. Questioning is not, therefore, merely one of the devices of teaching, it is really the whole of teaching. It is the excitation of the self-activities to their work of discovering truth. Nature always teaches thus. But is does not follow that every question should be in the interrogative form. The strongest and clearest affirmation may have all the effect of the interrogation, if the mind so receives it. An explanation may be so given as to raise new questions while it answers old ones.

28. The explanation that settles everything and ends all questions, usually ends all thinking also. After a truth is clearly understood, or a fact or principle established, there still remain its consequences, applications, and uses. Each fact and truth thoroughly studied leads to other facts which renew the questioning and demand fresh investigation. The alert and scientific mind is one that never ceases to ask questions and seek answers. The scientific spirit is the spirit of tireless inquiry and research. The present time, so far excelling the past in the development of its arts and sciences, is the time of great questions.

29. As with the world, so with the child. His education begins as soon as he begins to ask questions. It is only when the questioning spirit has been fully awakened, and the habit of raising questions has been largely developed, that the teaching process may embody the lecture plan. The truth asks its own questions as soon as the mind is sufficiently awake. The falling apple had the question of gravitation in it for the mind of Newton; and the boiling teakettle propounded to Watt the problem of a steam engine.

30. Like our other laws, this one also suggests some practical rules for teaching.

Rules for Teachers

(1) Adapt lessons and assignments to the ages and attainments of the pupils. Very young children will be interested more in whatever appeals to the senses, and especially in activities; the more mature will be attracted to reasoning and to reflective problems.

(2) Select lessons which relate to the environment and needs of the pupils.

(3) Consider carefully the subject and the lesson to be taught, and find its point of contact with the lives of your pupils.

(4) Excite the pupil's interest in the lesson when it is assigned, by some question or by some statement which will awaken inquiry. Hint that

something worth knowing is to be found out if the lesson is thoroughly studied, and then be sure later to ask for the truth to be discovered.

(5) Place yourself frequently in the position of a pupil among your pupils, and join in the search for some fact or principle.

(6) Repress your impatience which cannot wait for the pupil to explain himself, and which tends to take his words out of his mouth. He will resent it, and will feel that he could have answered had you given him time.

(7) In all class exercises aim to excite constantly fresh interest and activity. Start questions for the pupils to investigate out of class. The lesson that does not culminate in fresh questions ends wrong.

(8) Observe each pupil to see that his mind is not wandering so as to forbid its activities being bent to the lesson in hand.

(9) Count it your chief duty to awaken the minds of your pupils, and do not rest until each child shows his mental activity by asking questions.

(10) Repress the desire to tell all you know or think about the lesson or subject; if you tell something by way of illustration or explanation, let it start a fresh question.

(11) Give the pupil time to think, after you are sure that his mind is actively at work, and encourage him to ask questions when puzzled.

(12) Do not answer too promptly the questions asked, but restate them, to give them greater force and breadth, and often answer with new questions to secure deeper thought.

(13) Teach pupils to ask *What? Why?* and *How?*—the nature, cause, and method of every fact or principle taught them; also *Where? When? By whom?* and *What of it?*—the place, time, actors, and consequences of events.

(14) Recitations should not exhaust a subject, but leave additional work to stimulate the thought and the efforts of the pupils.

31. Many a teacher neglecting these rules kills all interest in his class, and wonders how he did it.

Violations and Mistakes

(1) The chief and almost constant violation of this law of teaching is the attempt to force lessons by simply telling. "I have told you ten times, and yet you don't know!" exclaims a teacher of this sort, who is unable to remember that knowing comes by thinking, not by being told.

(2) It is another mistake to complain of memory for not keeping what it never held. If facts or principles are to be remembered, the attention must be concentrated upon them at the time, and there must be a conscious effort to remember.

(3) A third violation of the law comes from the haste with which teachers require prompt and rapid recitations in the very words of the book; and, if a question is asked in class, to refuse the pupils time to think. If the pupil hesitates and stops

for lack of thought, or in apparent lack of memory, the fault lies in yesterday's teaching which shows its fruit today; but if it comes from the slowness of the pupil's thinking, or from the real difficulty of the subject, then time should be given for additional thought; and, if the recitation period will not permit it, let the answer hold over until the next time.

32. It is to this hurried and unthinking lesson-saying that we owe the superficial and impractical character of so much of our teaching. Instead of learning thoroughly the material of our lessons, we endeavor to learn them only so as to recite them promptly. If faults of this character are pr v-alent in our day schools, how much more serious are they in the Sunday schools? If the lessons of the Sunday schools are to carry over into the lives of the pupils by purifying and exalting their thoughts and making them wise in the religious beliefs taught them, the instruction must not be mere telling, but must be accompanied by the better methods used in the regular schools.

33. How different are the results when this great law of teaching is properly followed! The stimulated self-activities operate in the correct manner, and the classroom is transformed under their power into a busy laboratory. The pupils become thinkers—discoverers. They master great truths, and apply them to the great questions of life. They invade new fields of knowledge. The teacher merely leads the march. Their reconnaissance becomes a conquest. Skill and power grow with their exercise. Through this process, the students find out what their minds are for, and become students of life.

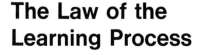

The Law of the Learning Process

1. We must now pass from the side of the teacher to that of the learner. It has been seen that the teacher's work consists essentially in arousing and guiding the self-activities of the pupils. The pupils' work, which we are now to consider, is the use of those self-activities in studying. The laws of teaching and learning may seem at first to be only different aspects of the same law, but they are really quite distinct—the one applying to the work of the instructor, the other to that of the one receiving the instruction. The law of the *teaching process* involves the means by which the self-activities are to be awakened; the law of the *learning process* determines the manner in which these activities shall be employed.

2. If we observe a child as he studies, and note carefully what he does, we shall easily see that it is not merely an effort of the attention nor a vague and purposeless exertion of his powers, that is required of him. There is a clear and distinct act or process which we wish him to accomplish.

It is to form in his own mind, by the use of his own powers, a true concept of the facts or principles in the lesson. This is the purpose to which all the efforts of teacher and pupil must be directed. The law of the learning process may therefore be stated thus: *The pupil must reproduce in his own mind the truth to be learned.*

3. With the laws previously discussed the teacher has been chiefly concerned; the law now before us concerns the pupil also. It brings into view the principles which must guide the student in his studying, and which it is the business of the instructor to emphasize and enforce. While telling the teacher how to teach, it also tells the pupil how to study.

The Philosophy of the Law

4. We have said that merely pouring out before pupils the content of the teacher's knowledge is not teaching. It should now be pointed out that true learning is not memorization and repetition of the words and ideas of the teacher. The work of education, contrary to common understanding, is much more the work of the pupil than of the teacher. This idea, which has been presented before in this discussion, is here reaffirmed as fundamental.

5. We must distinguish between the original discovery of a truth and learning it from others. Discovery is made by processes of original investigation and research which are usually slow, tentative, and laborious. Learning comes by processes of interpretation, which may be easy and rapid. Still there is much in common; the learner rediscovers in part the material that he learns. No real learning is wholly a repetition of the thoughts of others. The discoverer borrows largely of facts known to others, and the student must add to what he studies from his own experience. His aim should be to become an independent searcher in the fields of knowledge, not merely a passive learner at the hands of others. Both the original investigator and the student must be seekers for new facts and principles, and both must aim to gain clear and distinct conceptions of them. It is indispensable that the student should become an investigator.

6. There are several phases of the learning process which should be carefully noted here in order that the full meaning of the law shall be seen and understood.

(1) A pupil is sometimes said to have learned the lesson when he has committed it to memory, and can repeat or recite it word for word. This is all that is attempted by many pupils, or required by such teachers as consider their work done if they can secure verbatim reproductions. Education would be cheap and easy if this were real learning and could be made to stay.

(2) It is an evident advance over the memorizing of words when the pupil has also an under-

standing of the thought. It is so much better that many teachers are tempted to care only for the thought, and so to inform their pupils. There is a danger here, for in many cases, as in the teaching of the lessons in the Bible, it is important to know and to remember the words.

(3) It is still better when the pupil can translate the thought accurately into his own or other words without detriment to the meaning. The one who can do this has advanced beyond the work of mere learning, and has placed himself in the attitude of a discoverer. He has learned to deal with his own thoughts as well as the thoughts of others. The capable teacher will recognize this, and will pardon possible crudeness of expression, while he encourages the pupil to more accurate thinking as a means to more accurate language.

(4) The pupil shows still greater progress when he begins to seek evidence of the statements which he studies. The one who can give a reason for the things he believes is a better student as well as a stronger believer than the one who believes but does not know why. The real student seeks proofs, and a large part of the work of a student of nature is to prove the things which he discovers. The student of the Bible ought to seek to find out for himself if these things are so. Even the youngest pupils will take a stronger hold of the truth if they can see a reason for it. In searching for proof, the student

encounters much knowledge on the way, like the mountain climber who finds the landscape always widening around him. The particular problem with which he is engaged is seen to be a part of the great empire of truth.

(5) A still higher and more fruitful stage of learning is found in the study of the uses and applications of knowledge. No lesson is fully learned until it is traced to its connections with the great working machinery of nature and of life. Every fact has its relation to life, and every principle its applications, and until these are known, facts and principles are idle. The practical relations of truth, and the forces which lie behind all facts, are never really understood until we apply our knowledge to some of the practical purposes of life and of thought. The boy who finds a use for what he has learned in his lesson becomes doubly interested and successful in his school work. What was idle knowledge becomes practical wisdom.

7. The learning process is not completed until this last stage has been reached. The other steps aid in illumining the understanding of the pupils as they progress in their work, but our law of the learning process demands this final stage, and to this purpose the efforts of the teacher and the pupils must constantly be directed.

8. The earnest student will be enabled, by

means of these steps, to watch his own progress with his work. He can ask these questions: What does the lesson say? What is its meaning? How can I express this meaning in my own language? Do I believe what the lesson tells me, and why? What is the good of it—how may I apply and use the knowledge which it gives?

9. It is true that many lessons are not learned with this comprehensive thoroughness, but this does not change the fact that no lesson is really learned until so understood and so mastered.

Limitations of the Law

10. We should consider two limitations to this law of learning. The first has to do with the age of the pupils. It should be remembered that the mental activity of young children lies close to the senses. Their knowledge of a lesson will be largely confined to the facts which appeal to the eye, or which can be illustrated to the senses. A little later the desire of pupils for activity and for carrying on some active enterprise may profitably be utilized in their training. As maturity is approached, young people think more and more about reasons, and the lessons which will appeal most to them will be the ones which ask reasons and which give conclusions.

11. Another limitation is one concerned with the different fields of human knowledge. In each branch of knowledge there are distinct evidences and applications, and therefore the operation of the law of the learning process will vary to meet conditions. The capable teacher will discover these differences, and will find the proper conditions of successful study of each.

12. Herman Krusi, one of the best of teachers because one of the most sympathetic students of childhood, said: "Every child that I have ever observed, during all my life, has passed through certain remarkable questioning periods which seem to originate from his inner being. After each had passed through the early time of lisping and stammering, into that of speaking, and had come to the questioning period, he repeated at every new phenomenon the question, 'What is that?' If for an answer he received the name of a thing, it completely satisfied him; he wished to know no more. After a number of months, a second state made its appearance, in which the child followed its first question with a second: 'What is there in it?' These questions had much interest for me, and I spent much reflection upon them. In the end it became clear to me that the child had struck out the right method for developing its thinking faculties." Krusi's questions belong chiefly to the first period of growth and education; in the later periods come other questions.

13. The rules which follow from this law are useful both for teacher and pupil.

Practical Rules for Teachers and Learners

(1) Help the pupil to form a clear idea of the work to be done.

(2) Warn him that the words of his lesson have been carefully chosen; that they may have peculiar meanings, which it may be important to find out.

(3) Show him that usually more things are implied than are said.

(4) Ask him to express, in his own words, the meaning of the lesson as he understands it, and to persist until he has the whole thought.

(5) Let the reason *why* be perpetually *asked* till the pupil is brought to feel that he is expected to give a reason for his opinions. But let him also clearly understand that reasons must vary with the nature of the material he is studying.

(6) Aim to make the pupil an independent investigator—a student of nature and a seeker after truth. Cultivate in him the habit of research.

(7) Help him to test his conceptions to see that they reproduce the truth taught, as far as his powers permit.

(8) Seek constantly to develop in pupils a profound regard for truth as something noble and enduring.

(9) Teach the pupils to hate shams and sophistries and to shun them.

Violations and Mistakes

14. The violations of this law of the learning process are perhaps the most common and most fatal of any in our school work. Since the work of learning is the very heart of school work, a failure here is a failure in all. Knowledge may be placed before the pupils in endless profusion and in the most attractive guise; teachers may pour out instruction without stint, and lessons may be learned and recited under all the pressure of the most effective discipline and of the most urgent apeals; but if this law is not followed, the attainments will fall short of their mark. Some of the more common mistakes are these:

(1) The pupil is left in the twilight of an imperfect and fragmentary mastery by a failure to think it into clearness. The haste to go on often precludes time for thinking.

(2) The language of the textbook is so insisted upon that the pupil has no incentive to try his own power of expression. Thus he is taught to feel that the words are everything, the meaning nothing. Students often learn the demonstrations of geometry by heart, and do not suspect that there is any meaning in them.

(3) The failure to insist upon original thinking by the pupils is one of the most common faults of our schools.

(4) Frequently no reason is asked for the statements in the lesson, and none is given. The pupil believes what the book says, because the book says it.

(5) The practical applications are persistently neglected. That the lesson has a use, is the last thought to enter the minds of many pupils.

15. Nowhere are these faults in teaching more

frequent or more serious than in the Sunday school. "Always learning, but never able to come to a knowledge of the truth," tells the sad story of many a Sunday school class. If that class be taught as our law prescribes, the results might be very different.

The Law of Review and Application

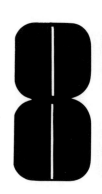

1. Let us suppose the process of teaching to be completed. The teacher and the pupils have met and have done their work together. Language freighted with ideas and aided with illustrations has been spoken and understood. Knowledge has been thought into the minds of the pupils, and it lies there in greater or less completeness, to feed thought, to guide and modify conduct, and to form character. What more is needed? The teacher's work seems ended. But difficult work yet remains, perhaps the most difficult. All that has been accomplished lies hidden in the minds of the pupils, and lies there as a potency rather than as a possession. What process shall fix into active habits the thought-potencies which have been evolved? What influence shall mold into permanent ideals the conceptions that have been gained? It is for this final and finishing work that our seventh and last law provides. This law of the confirmation and ripening of results, may be expressed as follows: *The completion, test and con-*

firmation of the work of teaching must be made by review and application.

2. The statement of this law seeks to include the chief aims of the review: (1) to perfect knowledge, (2) to confirm knowledge, and (3) to render this knowledge ready and useful. These three aims, though distinct in idea, are so connected in fact as to be secured by the same process. It would be difficult to overstate the value and importance of this law of review. No time in teaching is spent more profitably than that spent in reviewing. Other things being equal, the ablest and most successful teacher is the one who secures from his pupils the most frequent, thorough, and interesting reviews.

The Philosophy of the Law

3. A review is more than a repetition. A machine may repeat a process, but only an intelligent agent can review it. The repetition done by a machine is a second movement precisely like the first; a repetition by the mind is the rethinking of a thought. It is necessarily a review. It is more: it involves fresh conceptions and new associations, and brings an increase of facility and power.

4. Reviews are of different grades of completeness and thoroughness, from the mere repetition of the words of lessons, or a rapid glance thrown back to some fact or phrase, to the most careful resurvey of the whole field—the occupancy in full force of the ground of which the first study was only a reconnaissance. The simplest reviews are mostly repetitions; the final and complete reviews should be thorough restudies of the lessons.

5. A partial review may embrace a single lesson, or it may include a single topic of the subject—the development of a single fact or principle, the recall of some event, or of some difficult point or question. The complete review may be a cursory reviewing of the whole field in a few general questions, or it may be a full and final reconsideration of the whole ground. Each kind of review has its place and use. We shall see in our discussion that no teaching can be complete without the review, made either under the teacher's direction, or voluntarily by the pupil himself.

6. A new lesson or a fresh topic never reveals all of itself at first. It distracts the attention and its novelties may dazzle the mind. When we enter a strange house we do not know where to look for its several rooms, and the attention is drawn to a few of the more singular and conspicuous pieces of furniture or articles of decoration. We must return again and again, and resurvey the scene with eyes grown familiar to the place, before the whole plan of the building and the uses of all the rooms and their furniture will stand clearly revealed. So one must return again and again to a lesson if he would see all there is in it, and come to a true and vivid understanding of its meaning. We have all noticed how much we find that is new and interesting in reading again some old and familiar volume.

7. Even in the best-studied book, we are often surprised to find fresh truths and new meanings in passages which we had read perhaps again and again. It is the ripest student of Shakespeare who finds the most freshess in the works of the great dramatist. The familiar eye discovers in any great masterpiece of art or literature touches of power and beauty which the casual observer cannot see. So a true review always adds something to the knowledge of the student who makes it.

8. Especially is this true of the Bible, of which the latest study is the richest and most interesting. Nothing more surprises or delights us in the great preachers than the new meanings they discover in old and familiar texts—meanings which clearly are there, but which we had not found in our own reading. Sometimes these meanings are hidden in a word, and need perhaps only the right emphasis to reveal them; sometimes they lie close by the path and appear by some sidelight thrown skilfully upon them by the text. Repetition with varying emphasis often may bring to light these hidden meanings.

9. On one occasion at least, the Great Teacher resorted to this power of repetition, when three times in succession He asked Peter the question,

"Lovest thou me?" The heart of the disciple burned under this powerful iteration, and with memory and conscience quickened he appealed to the Master to witness to the truth of his questioned love.

10. But the repetitions of a review are not made the same hour. They are spread over days and weeks, and hence a new element is brought into play. The lapse of time changes the point of view. At every review we survey the lesson from a new standpoint. Its facts rise in a new order and are seen in new relations. Truths that were overshadowed in the first study now come forth into the light. When one climbs a mountain, from each successive outlook the eye visits again the same landscape, but the position of the observer is always changed. The features of the landscape are seen in different perspective, and each successive view is larger, more comprehensive, and more complete than its predecessor.

11. The human mind does not achieve its victories by a single effort. There is a sort of mental incubation as a result of which some splendid discovery oftentimes springs forth. The physiologists call it unconscious cerebration, by which they mean that the brain itself goes on working unknown to us. It is an easier explanation that the evergrowing mind reaches constantly new positions, and obtains new light by which a new truth becomes visible. Some fresh experience or newly acquired idea serves as a key to the old lesson, and what was dark in the first study is made clear and bright in the review.

12. The old saying, "Beware of the man of one book," has this in it, that his repeated readings of his one book give him a mastery of the subject which makes him a dangerous antagonist in his chosen field. He shows the power conferred by frequent reviews.

13. Frequent repetitions are valuable to correct memorization and ready recall. Memory depends upon the association of ideas—the idea in mind recalling the ideas with which it has been linked by some past association. Each review establishes new associations, while at the same time it familiarizes and strengthens the old. The lesson that is studied but once is likely learned only to be forgotten. That which is thoroughly and repeatedly reviewed is woven into the very fabric of our thoughts, and becomes a part of our equipment of knowledge. Not what a pupil has once learned and recited, but what he permanently remembers and uses is the correct measure of his achievement.

14. Not merely to know, but to have knowledge for use—to possess it fully, like money for daily expenditures, or tools and materials for daily work—such is the aim of true study. This readiness of knowledge cannot be gained by a single study. Frequent and thorough reviews can alone give this firm hold and free handling of the truth. There is a skill in scholarship as well as in handicraft, and this skill in both cases depends upon habits; and habit is the child of repetition.

15. The plastic power of truth in shaping conduct and molding character belongs only to the truths which have become familiar by repetitions. Not the scamper of a passing child but the repeated tread of coming and going feet beats for us the paths of our daily life. If we would have any great truth sustain and control us, we must return to it so often that it will at last rise up in mind as a dictate of conscience, and pour its steady light upon every act and purpose with which it is concerned.

16. The well known influence of maxims and proverbs comes from the readiness with which they are remembered and recalled, and the power which they gather by repetition. The Scriptural texts which most influence us are those that have become familiar in use, and which arise in mind as occasions demand.

17. From all this it will be seen that the review is not simply an added excellence in teaching which may be dispensed with if time is lacking; it is one of the essential conditions of all true teaching. Not to review is to leave the work half done. The law of review rests upon the laws of mind. The review may not always be made formally and with clear design, but no successful teaching was ever done in which the review in some form, either by direction of the teacher or by the private impulse of the learner, did not take place—the revisiting and repetition of the lesson that had been learned. The "line upon line and precept upon precept" rule of the Bible is a recognition of this truth.

18. The processes of review must necessarily vary with the subject of study, and also with the age and advancement of the pupils. With very young pupils the review can be little more than simple repetition; with older pupils, the review will be a thoughtful restudy of the ground to gain deeper understanding.

19. A principle in mathematics may be reviewed with fresh applications and problems. A scientific principle may be fixed by the study or analysis of a fresh specimen, or by additional facts in support of the same principle. A chapter in history may be restudied with fresh questions calling for a fresh view, or by comparing it with the new statements of another author. A Scriptural truth will be reviewed by a new application to the heart and conscience or to the judgment of the duties and events of the life.

20. In the Bible more than in any other book

are reviews needful and valuable. Not only does the Bible most require and most repay repeated study, but most of all ought Bible knowledge to be familiar to us. Its words and precepts should rest clear and precise in the thought as the dictates of duty.

21. Any exercise may serve as a review which recalls the material to be reviewed. One of the best and most practical forms of review is the calling up of any fact or truth learned and applying it to some use. Nothing so fixes it in the memory or gives such a grasp of it to the understanding. Thus the multiplication table may be learned by orderly repetitions of its successive factors and products, but its frequent review and use in daily computations alone give us that perfect mastery of it which makes it come without call. So in that largest, most wonderful, and most perfect acquisition of the human mind—the thousands of wholly artificial word-signs and idioms of the mother tongue—nothing but the ceaseless repetitions and reviews of daily use could so imbed them in the memory and so work them into the habitudes of the mind that they come with the ideas that they symbolize and keep pace with the swift movements of thought itself, as if a natural part of the thinking process.

22. The ready skill of artisans and professional men in recalling instantaneously the principles and processes of their arts or professions is the product of the countless repetitions of daily practice. This kind of review is available in all cases where the pupil can be called upon to apply the material learned to the solution of common problems, the conduct of any process, or the performance of any series of acts. The art of the teacher, in this work, lies in the stating of questions which shall properly make use of the material to be reviewed.

23. The use of handwork in review ought by no means to be neglected. The hand is itself a capable teacher, and few reviews are more effective than those which are aided by the hand. Witness the power and value of laboratory work, now so common in all scientific study.

24. The request for the pupils to bring lists of persons, objects, places, etc., mentioned in the lessons, for tabular statements of facts or events, for maps, plans, or drawings of places or things, or for short written statements or answers, will be of valuable assistance in reviewing.

Practical Rules for Teachers

25. Among the many practical rules for review, the following are some of the most useful:

(1) Consider reviews as always in order.

(2) Have set times for review. At the beginning of each period review briefly the preceding lesson.

(3) At the close of each lesson, glance backward at the ground which has been covered. Al-

most every good lesson closes with a summary. It is well to have the pupils know that any one of them may be called upon to summarize the lesson at the close of the class period.

(4) After five or six lessons, or at the close of a topic, take a review from the beginning. The best teachers give about one-third of each period to purpose of review. Thus they make haste slowly but progress surely.

(5) Whenever a reference to former lessons can profitably be made, the opportunity thus afforded to bring old knowledge into fresh light should be seized.

(6) All new lessons should be made to bring into review and application the material of former lessons.

(7) Make the first review as soon as practicable after the lesson is first learned.

(8) In order to make reviews easily and rapidly, the teacher should hold in mind the material that has been learned, in large units or blocks, ready for instant use. He is thus able to begin at any time an impromptu review in any part of the field. The pupils, seeing that the teacher thinks it worth while to remember and recall what has been studied, will desire to do the same, and will be ambitious to be ready to meet his questions.

(9) New questions on old lessons, new illustrations for old texts, new proof for old statements, new applications of old truths, will often

send the pupil back with fresh interest to his old material, thus affording a profitable review.

(10) The final review, which should never be omitted, should be searching, comprehensive, and masterful, grouping the different topics of the subject as on a map, and aiding the pupil to a familiar mastery of the material which he has learned.

(11) *Find as many applications as possible.* Every thoughtful application involves a useful and effective review.

(12) Do not forget the value of handwork in review.

(12) Do not forget the value of handwork on the material of previous lessons. Let this be done frequently; the pupils will soon learn to come to their classes with questions ready to ask, and with ready answers for other questions.

Violations and Mistakes

26. The common and almost constant violations of this law of teaching are well known to every one. But the disastrous violations are known only to those who have considered thoughtfully the inadequate and stinted outcomes of much of our laborious and costly teaching. The lack of proper review is not by any means the sole cause of failure; however, a wider and more thorough use of the principle of review would go far to remedy the evils from other causes. We pour water into broken cisterns; good reviews might not at once increase the quantity of water which goes in, but they would stop the leaks.

(1) The first violation of the law is the total neglect of review. This is the folly of the utterly poor teacher.

(2) The second is the wholly inadequate review. This is the fault of the hurried and impatient teacher who is often more concerned with getting through the work of the term or semester than making the work the pupils' own.

(3) The third mistake is that of delaying all review work until the end of the semester or term, when, the material of the course being largely forgotten, the review amounts to little more than a poor relearning, with little interest and less value.

(4) The fourth error is that of making the review merely a process of lifeless and colorless repetition of questions and answers and often the very questions and answers which were originally used. This is a review in name only.

27. The law of review in its full force and philosophy requires that there shall be fresh vision —a clear rethinking and reusing of the material which has been learned, which shall be related to the first study as the finishing touches of the artist to his first sketches.

28. We have now finished our discussion of the seven laws of teaching. If we have succeeded in our purpose, our readers have seen: *first,* the true

Conclusion

teacher, equipped with the knowledge he wishes to communicate; *second,* the pupil, with attention fixed and interest aroused eager to pursue his studies; *third,* the true medium of communication between the two—a language clear, simple, and easily understood by both; *fourth,* the true lesson, the knowledge or experience to be communicated. These four, the actors and the machinery of the drama, have been shown in action, giving, *fifth,* the true teaching process, the teacher arousing and directing the self-activities of the pupils; *sixth,* the true learning process, the pupils reproducing in their own thought, step by step—first in mere outline and finally in full and finished conception—the lesson to be learned; and *seventh,* the true review, testing, correcting, completing, connecting, confirming, and applying the subject studied. In all this there has been seen only the working of the great natural laws of mind and truth effecting and governing that complex process by which a human intelligence gains possession of knowledge. The study of these laws may not make of every reader a perfect teacher; but the laws themselves, when fully observed in use, will produce their effects with the same certainty that chemical laws generate the compounds of chemical elements, or that the laws of life produce the growth of the body.